It's Monday Morning:
"There Are People In My Office Working . . .and I'm Not One of Them"

Realities of Retirement

James P. O'Brien

© 2015

**It's Monday Morning: "There Are People in My Office Working. . .
. . . and I'm Not One of Them!"**

Realities of Retirement

Preface

One of these days not far in the future, it will be another Monday. There will be people in your office working and you will not be one of them. Unless you are sick or playing hooky, you will be retired. Congratulations.

Whether you are 25, 35, 45, 55 or 65, retirement is inevitable. It will happen if you live long enough, even if you say: "I'm never going to retire!" Maybe you have been thinking about retirement already. Everyone does, sooner or later.

Will you be ready? If you are 25, it is a good time to begin planning. Forty-two years from now, you will be glad and envied. If you are 35 or 45, time is shorter but you have years to implement a savings plan, even though the magic of compounding will not work as well as when you were younger. If you are reading this at 50, there is not much time to prepare if you have not already but you still can do it. There would be nothing worse than to be retired and lack the financial resources to support yourself.

Few Americans are doing much to prepare for their retirement. Only 48 percent of American employees have an idea what they will need to support themselves in retirement. [1] In 2015, people over 65 are 13% of the USA population and this figure is dramatically increasing because we are living longer. [2] Nonetheless, 1/3 have nothing saved for retirement. [3] They will have to depend on Social Security, which is not a savings plan; it is a government entitlement program.

The M.s had dreamed of buying a small fifth-wheel trailer in retirement to travel extensively, particularly to the Sun Belt during cold winter months. F., an auto salesperson, and D., homemaker, both recently turned 65 and applied for Social Security benefits. Although they had

---

[1] http://www.fool.com/retirement/general/2015/10/25/how-much-income-will-i-need-in-retirement.aspx
[2] http://money.usnews.com/money/retirement/articles/2012/01/09/65-and-older-population-soars
[3] http://www.usnews.com/news/articles/2014/08/18/more-than-one-third-of-americans-have-no-savings

received annual statements detailing F.'s benefits should he retire, they ignored these, either filing them or simply trashing. Last year, when retirement became eminent, they realized that his monthly benefit was only going to be $946 while her spousal benefit would be $473, a total of $1419 per month, or $17,028 per year. This is less than half of their pre-retirement salary from F.'s position with the auto dealership. They have no savings. They cannot afford to travel and they cannot afford a trailer.

Attitudes toward money depend on one's generation. There are various schemes for categorizing Americans by age: [4]

- G.I. Generation   born 1900-1924
- Silent Generation (Lucky Few)   born 1925-1945
- Baby Boomers   born 1946-1964
- Generation X   born 1965-1979
- Minnennials or Generation Y   born 1980-2000

Each generation has different attitudes, not only to money and saving, but to work ethic, relationships, commitment, change, authority and learning. [5] As far as money, the G.I. Generation, if any are still alive, were children of the Great Depression, [6] who lived with poverty and unemployment. They are the ones who turned off an electric light when they left a room. The Silent Generation, born between wars or during World War II, were equally thrifty and, if still alive, are enjoying their retirement. Baby Boomers, the youngest of whom will retire in 2016 at age 67, are spenders and borrowers, who hope money will be there when they need it. Gen X's are entrepreneurial and believe ideas can be turned into money. Unlike Boomers, who were corporate people, Gen X's are likely to be small business owners. And Minnennials, the children of Boomers, have always

---

[4] http://geography.about.com/od/populationgeography/qt/generations.htm
[5] http://www.napavalley.edu/people/jhall/Documents/Generational%20Chart.pdf
[6] http://www.history.com/topics/great-depression

had money and are willing to pay the price for alleged quality. In a word, the defining label for each generation, respectively, could be: [7]

- Deprivation
- Frugality
- Individuality
- Cynicism
- Entitlement

How does each generation plan and save for retirement? There is no magic to saving. You simply make the commitment to do so and follow through. You live on less than you make and save the difference. If you do not, retirement will be dismal.

Can you afford the lifestyle you are presently living? Can you also save 10-15% of your earnings for retirement? If you cannot and do not, then you will not be ready to retire. Even if you have several years before you retire, time is short. It may be time to live below, not beyond, your means and save for tomorrow. Social Security will be there, but it will undoubtedly change as years pass. Even now, it would be difficult to live on benefits from this entitlement program alone, although 22% of all married couples and 47% of singles depend on Social Security for 90% of their retirement income. [8] If benefits are reduced, and this is possible, it will become even more difficult. In addition, the retirement age has transitioned to 67 and may be lengthened for full benefits in future decades.

This book is not about early retirement. No one is certain what early retirement is. Rather, it is about timely retirement. Although it would be nice to retire at age 30, it is a loss of productivity to society. Better to live your life and fulfill your job or career for 30-40 years and then reap the joys of retirement. The slogan is not: "Eat, drink and be merry for tomorrow you die!" Rather, it is: "Eat, drink and be merry with restraint, for tomorrow you retire and will need what you have saved!"

---

[7] *Ibid.*
[8] https://www.ssa.gov/news/press/basicfact.html

Beyond the rudiments of financing retirement, there are other issues. What are the financial realities of retirement? How will you deal with income flows and expenses? Are there tax advantages and consequences to being retired? And what will you do in retirement? Do you have burning passions yet to fulfill or do you plan to become a couch potato and watch daytime TV talk shows? Where are you going to live and how? Will you change homes in the city in which you live or even change cities? If you have been working for 40 years, you probably have not been around your partner that much. Will you be able to get along with your spouse? What are lifestyle options? And how do you live well within your means, that is, how can you live on the cheap? And finally, do you plan to save or spend your children's inheritance? What is gifting and what effect could estate taxes have on your heirs?

Let those people continue to work in your office on Monday morning after you retire. Let them work every weekday until it is their turn to retire. Your departure will leave as much of a hole in the organization as remains when you withdraw your hand from a bucket of water. Your co-workers will say they miss you but they secretly will wish they were not in that office on Monday either. They will have their chance to enjoy what you will be enjoying when it is their time. You can even share this book with them.

This book is written for anyone who will eventually retire. It is based on fact and personal experience of the author, who has spent a career thinking and planning for retirement but never obsessing about it. Retirement is inevitable. Let us plan for it. This book should help you do so realistically in the years you have before you leave the work force.

The M.s have just realized each will have $104.90 [9] deducted (2015) from their monthly FICA checks for Part B of Medicare. F. will be dropped from the group health insurance program where he was employed and they will need to find a gap-insurance to cover the difference between what Medicare covers and what health care will cost.

---

[9] https://www.medicare.gov/your-medicare-costs/costs-at-a-glance/costs-at-glance.html

They will undoubtedly have extra premiums deducted should they elect the Medicare Prescription Drug Program [10] from a qualified provider. Although their modest home will be paid off soon after retirement, there will be utilities, insurance and property taxes to pay, ever spiraling upward the longer they live. Their benefits from Social Security will probably not be taxed, [11] but the difference will not compensate for the disparity between what they earned and what they will have in retirement. Their dreams and goals may have to be changed or be left unfulfilled.

---

[10] https://en.wikipedia.org/wiki/Medicare_Part_D
[11] https://faq.ssa.gov/link/portal/34011/34019/Article/3831/Must-I-pay-taxes-on-Social-Security-benefits

Chapter One

Leaving the Workforce: Are you ready to retire?

Although he was able to sleep later now, K. still had misgivings about retirement. Some mornings, in that twilight zone between sleep and wakefulness, he mused to himself: "I used to be so young!" He would swing out of bed, a bit slowly and with a few pains, now fully awake, and say: "Well, I'm sure not young anymore."

If you are worried about being older, are you ready to retire? Really ready, not just thinking about it. You are going to get older, whether or not you retire. Many older folks still in the workforce chat about retiring around the water cooler or copy machine and share dreams about how it will be. Even younger workers boast they are going to retire "by the time I'm 35!"

Are you ready to retire? How will you know? Is there a "right" age to retire? When will your verbal declarations translate into a solid strategic plan to enable you to have a rich, fulfilling lifestyle beyond the traditional workforce? And can you live outside the workforce?

What is the traditional workforce? For purposes of retirement, it means anyone who works in some capacity for themselves or others to earn money for support. It can be factory worker, restaurant server, medical doctor, receptionist, salesperson, attorney, retail clerk, agricultural worker, real estate broker, teacher, bartender, judge, beautician, stock broker, fast food worker or manager, small-business owner, farmer, corporate CEO, and on and on. If you receive money on a periodic basis for a service or product you deliver, you are part of the traditional workforce. In the United States, it includes

149,120,000 people employed and 7,908,000 looking for jobs, a total potential of 157,080,000 in October 2015. [12]

Excluded are folks who work without compensation, such as homemaker, stay-at-home mom or dad, or volunteer caregiver. You cannot retire in the traditional sense if you have not been paid for your efforts, even though you have a social contract with a spouse, partner or your family, which enables or requires you to work without monetary compensation. An empty nester is not a retiree; he or she is an empty nester. If you "work at home", you are not part of the traditional workforce even though your service is necessary and valued. If you "work outside the home" or "work from home" and receive compensation for it, then you are part of the traditional workforce.

> *When K. and M. were married right after college graduation thirty-five years ago, M. worked two years until the birth of their first child. Since it was more costly for daycare than her job provided, they agreed she would stay at home and raise the kids while K. climbed the corporate ladder at the engineering firm. It worked well and their four children have had happy and healthy home lives in which both parents participated. Now their friends are throwing a party to celebrate their retirements. But M. insists that only K. is retiring.*

We will exclude folks who exit the workforce and then return, perhaps several times during their potential earning years. These people are not retired. They're on sabbatical or vacation. Another exclusion is people who are forced to retire. In reality, they are not retired. They are unemployed and had little opportunity to develop a retirement plan. This is true, even if the reason is medical. In this book, retirement is defined as a willful separation from work on a voluntary basis with the thought of never working again, at least, fulltime.

---

[12] http://www.dlt.ri.gov/lmi/laus/us/usadj.htm

Age-based Retirement: How will you know when you're ready to retire? Maybe you have reached "retirement age", whatever that means. For a company, it can be 30 years of service. Maybe you have reached the 65 years plus "x" months required by Social Security if you were born after 1937. [13] It could mean you cannot drive to work anymore because you failed the eye exam for your drivers' license on your 79th birthday. Perhaps you have accumulated enough wealth at age 41 to call it quits. It might mean your trust fund, endowed by generous grandparents, has kicked in because you turned 25.

Is there such a thing as "early" retirement? Probably not, unless your decision is made at 5:30 a.m. Although you might decide to apply for Social Security at age 62 or to separate from your company before you reach 55, these are willful acts, not early retirement. As with all decisions, they carry costs and benefits. There is no "normal" retirement age but there certainly can be premature retirement, if it is done before one has counted the costs, weighed the risks and assessed the advantages.

Emotion-based Retirement: Nonetheless retirement is typically age-based. You do it when you are older. Other workers of similar age are also retiring. But equally importantly, it is psychologically based. You do it when you are ready! You do it when you have had enough of the workforce. Although you may love your job and the people you work with, the projects are no longer important, at least to you. You get tired of the 8 to 5 grind as well as the daily commute. You are tired of picking up take-out food on the way home so your family is fed. It might mean departmental meetings are meaningless and your boss is a Neanderthal. Perhaps younger people in your organization have more influence, even though you have the experience. Your boss might be 30 years younger than you. Maybe it means you are ready to do something different, perhaps nothing.

Unit meetings on Monday mornings ceased to hold any magic for A. at the realty firm. Updates on mortgage rates and escrow fees did not translate into meaningful application for her clients. Furthermore, the

---

[13] https://www.socialsecurity.gov/planners/retire/agereduction.html

market was glutted with over-priced homes sought by buyers with low FICOS who did not qualify for these properties. There was a new broker as well. And the motivation of being a million-dollar salesperson was no longer enticing. Her 401k was doing well and her parents had just left her a nice bundle of money. It was time to stop being a realtor. It was time to retire.

Even though you believe you are ready to retire, does your job define who you are? If your self-concept and self-esteem are all work-related, will you be happy outside the workforce? If the power, influence and prestige you enjoy in the work environment define you, you may find that no longer being the office manager, being addressed as "Dr", "Boss", "Chairperson", "Principal", "Team Leader", "Ms.", "Reverend", "Administrative Associate", "Senator", "Your Honor" or even just being the gate-keeper for information will leave you totally unprepared for retirement. In retirement, everyone becomes a P.I.P. (Previously Important Person). If you can survive being unimportant, you may be ready for retirement. If you never were important (P.U.P., Previously Unimportant Person), then you will love it.

On some mornings, K.'s musing while awakening was: "I used to be so important." But then it struck him as he became fully awake and swung out of bed. His inner voice reminded him: "What do you mean? You were never important!"

Chronological age and mental set are the two ingredients that define if you are ready. There are twenty-five year olds in the workforce who are psychologically ready but they have not paid their dues. Humans were made to work most of their lifetimes. Jobs and careers should span 30, 40 or more years of our adult lives. Sixty-five years of age seemed like a reasonable retirement age when FDR signed Social Security[14] into existence in the 1930's. With increased life expectancy, retirement age exceeds that

---

[14] https://en.wikipedia.org/wiki/Social_Security_Act

arbitrary age for many. Our professions might involve us for well over a half-century of our lives.

Finance-based Retirement: Regardless of age and mental readiness, there has to be a solid financial plan to provide income so that you can afford to retire. It cannot occur just because you are older and burned out. Money must support your needs and wants when the steady income flow from employment ceases. This has traditionally been a three-pronged pool of funds: (1) personal savings; (2) company pension or 401k plan; and (3) Social Security. Many pundits have stated that you need 70%[15] of your pre-retirement income in order to retire, since 30% is consumed through your job and will not be needed once you stop working.

Can you live on 70% of your pre-retirement income when you retire? Or 60%? Or 80%? Probably not. This is old-style thinking that assumed you would retire debt-free. This means your house and car are paid off and you have no consumer debt, such as credit card balances or college loans for your children. The 70% rule would then have some validity. Most employees take 60-65% of their gross pay home, the amount that is not consumed through federal and state taxes, retirement and medical deductions, or union and professional dues. Although you may be in a lower tax bracket, taxes do not end because of retirement. Neither will medical insurance premiums, but you may be in a better risk group when you retire. Professional dues and payments into 401ks and retirement accounts will cease since you will now be drawing upon those funds, not paying into them. With this considerations, you may find that achieving 70% of retirement income much less daunting.

Many people do not have their home paid off at retirement. In America, only 1/3 of homes are mortgage-free,[16] except in high-priced markets, such as regions of California or New York, where only one out of five homes is free and clear. An average

---

[15] http://www.consumerismcommentary.com/do-you-need-80-of-your-current-income-in-retirement/

[16] http://articles.latimes.com/2013/jan/10/business/la-fi-free-and-clear-20130110

homeowner remains in a house 5-7 years [17] and 2/3 of owners typically sell owing on their mortgage. In addition, debt-load for seniors has more than doubled in the last 15 years, [18] due to spending habits, wage stagnation and the generational attitude towards money.

> *K. and his spouse L. had both worked for over 30 years in their chosen professions, she as a CPA which prepared payroll and taxes for several small business on a contractual basis, he as a high school math teacher and part-time coach. Although L. had been able to keep her contracts going during childbearing and raising years, she does not have the public pension that K. enjoys. Nonetheless, they are relatively debt-free, except for two more years to pay on their mortgage. Their replacement income in retirement is almost 90% of what they had while in the workforce. Once the home is paid off, they will have ample income to support their retirement goals and interests.*

In addition to home ownership, the argument is advanced that 30% of your budget comes from work related expense, such as clothes and commuting. Thus, 70% should be sufficient. This is probably not true. Unless you have a position where you purchase designer clothes frequently, 30% reduction is not realistic. Neither can fuel costs and parking fees nor the convenience of sending laundry out, dining in restaurants or eating take-out food account for it. The 30% can only be attributed to housing and car costs that have been paid off before or at retirement or to your higher income tax bracket, deductions for retirement plans and professional dues, as cited above.

If you are going to live as you did before retirement, with the same mortgage, car payments, consumer debt payments and utilities, you need 100% of your pre-retirement income to support yourself. This assumes that you're not going to live differently either.

---

[17] http://www.homeinsight.com/details.asp?url_id=7
[18] http://www.usatoday.com/story/money/personalfinance/2013/03/21/census-household-debt-report/2007195/

It is the premise of this book, however, that you will need 130% of pre-retirement to retire in a secure, exciting manner, unless you want to spend your golden years watching daytime talk shows on television. This buffer allows you to pursue new activities, to travel and to purchase goods and services that will enhance your newly achieved freedom. It is a lofty goal, but it can be attained.

Being ready to retire means you have reached an age where many co-workers do retire, you want to separate from the workforce and you have the financial resources to support yourself for the next 30 to 40 years with 70%, 100% or 130% of your pre-retirement income.

As career teachers from New York State, T. and K. were "pre-programmed" toward retirement at age 55. Some of their colleagues stayed longer, especially those who had never developed outside interests. They heard many retirement "experts", including those from the NYS Retirement System, explain that beyond 55, they would actually be paying their school district to work in terms of real dollars. K. wanted to "make up" the year and a half she took for an eighteen-month maternity leave, and she said she was not "ready yet" when she turned 55.

From a financial standpoint, T. and K. knew they would be on solid ground with pensions from the NYSTRS. They both qualified (based on years of service and a modest "incentive") for 70% of their final average salaries for their last three years of service. In addition, to offset inflation over a long retirement, they began contributing to 403b tax shelter plans early in their careers. Almost every time they received a contractual raise, they would try to budget so they could put an additional 50-75% of the raise into the tax shelters. That nest egg grew nicely, in spite of some losses in recessions of recent years. The tax shelter plans also allowed both to opt for the "maximum" plan in their pensions. If one pre-deceases the other, the 403b's are there to make up the difference. Fortunately in NYS, retiree medical benefits are a contractual item by school district. Theirs is based on un-used sick days, and they both have very good medical/dental plans, which will carry them without cost to Medicare days.

Here is a comprehensive way of looking at these main points:

Debt situation	Retirement activity	% needed
House and cars paid off	Want to do nothing extra	70%
House and cars paid off	Want to do exciting things	100%
House and cars **not** paid off	Want to do nothing extra	100%
House and cars **not** paid off	Want to do exciting things	130%

These percentages are guidelines but will be used as norms throughout this book to describe pre-retirement situations. If your house payments are low because you have held a mortgage for a long-time, the figures (percentages) may not reflect your situation. Similarly, if you have a large mortgage on your home as well as a home equity loan, the figures may not be applicable either. The duration of loans on house or car may also determine where you fall in this chart. A mortgage that pays out in a year or so is quite different from one which has another ten or fifteen years to zero out. Assess your financial commitment and retirement motivation before jumping into a situation you cannot support because of long-term debt.

And if you have several years to plan and save before you retire, you easily can achieve these goals.

A, computer programmer and mathematician, had this to say about retirement: "I decided to retire eighteen years ago after we moved because I then had to commute through three traffic jams instead of one. My spouse was semi-retired and could work from home. I was old enough at 55 to retire with full benefits. Some people say they miss the people but not the job. Not so with me. I missed the job, the feeling of self-worth and the feeling of accomplishment. I felt guilty going to the tennis courts in the morning instead of the office! My advice is this: 'Do not retire unless you are sure you are ready.' Even then it can be difficult. Plan ahead what you will do. Although, I did, it still took more than six months to adjust."

Summary: Here is a checklist to help you decide. If you can answer "Yes" to each of these issues, you are ready to retire.

Issue	Yes	No
Are many people my age and in my employment retiring?		
Is retirement my willful choice? (That is, Do I want to retire?)		
Will I enjoy being a *P.I.P or a **P.U.P?		
Do I have the 3 pools of personal savings, company pension and Social Security benefits to support my retirement?		
Does the percentage (70%, 100% or 130%) of the pre-retirement income I will have available realistically reflect my financial situation and retirement goals?		

*Previously Important Person

**Previously Unimportant Person

Chapter Two

Your Financial Planning: Can you afford to retire?

T. and C. are retiring.   They both turn 60 in the New Year and are simply tired of working. T. has been employed in refineries for most of his adult life, ever since high school. He has elevated his position and salary by developing skills needed in the petroleum industry and presently runs a large crew of men. Through bust and boom, he has been an oilman.

C., on the other hand, has worked intermittently since she married T. almost 35 years ago. She was out of the workforce for over fifteen years when their two children were in school. For the past several years, she has been an office manager for a real estate broker.

Their combined income has been modest but they have about $85,000 in savings, mostly invested in mutual funds, money market and CDs, as well as $16,500 in IRAs.   They will not be eligible for Social Security benefits for another two years and may not take it until they can receive full benefits. They have not really "run the numbers" on what they will have in retirement but just want to quit working.   As T. said to C.: "Whatever money we have, we'll just get by. We will make it work! After all, our house is almost paid for."

The traditional mentality of "we'll get by" is neither appropriate nor sufficient in retirement planning.   Since your retirement years will be decades long, the financial situation has to drive your decision.[19]   Regardless of your age, you can still work out a solid financial plan to support your goals if you begin now. If you were to retire at 65 years of age after thirty years in your job or profession, it is possible you will live to be

---

[19] http://life-span.healthgrove.com/l/61/60

85 or more. [20] The average American worker lives 20 years after retirement. [21] Will you have the funds to support those years of retirement? Will your pool of funds grow to keep up with inflation? This is critical if your partner or spouse has never worked outside the home. One employment income does not translate into two retirement incomes.

Most people do not begin saving early enough to develop the three pools of funds for retirement. This book is not designed to provide a "magic bullet" for people. There is no "magic bullet" to save more. You cannot afford to retire unless you have personal savings, that is, unless you want a lower standard of living.   If you are not saving and you are 25 or 35 or 45 or 55, then begin. You should commit between 10-15% [22] of your income to personal savings.   The older you are, the more you need to accumulate over a shorter duration.   How to do it is not the issue; the amount you have accumulated and how to plug it into your retirement income is.

There are three pools of funds that are critical to your retirement:

1. **Personal savings**: Money you voluntarily pay yourself and preserve only for retirement;
2. **Company pension**, 401ks, 403bs, 457s, SEPs and IRAs: Money you may or are required to pay yourself by your employer; and
3. **Social Security**: Tax you pay into the Federal government general fund, which provides an I.O.U. of potential future benefits.

Personal Savings. Personal savings can be bank accounts or CDs (certificates of deposit.) There are investments in real estate that can be liquidated when you need the cash. Your home is personal savings. Should you sell it when you retire, you have a pool of cash. This pool depends on the home's value as well as your equity. If it is

---

[20] https://data.oecd.org/healthstat/life-expectancy-at-65.htm
[21] http://www.superlife.co.nz/how-long-might-i-live-for-in-retirement.html
[22] http://www.investopedia.com/articles/personal-finance/092414/retirement-what-percentage-salary-save.asp

mortgage-free, your pool of cash could be considerable. You will not have a place to live if you sell your house. But it is conceivable you might sell a larger home and replace it will a smaller one, using the cash difference as a savings pool to support retirement. You might also rent an apartment, thus saving on taxes, insurance and maintenance.

There are several ways to manage your pool of cash. Let's assume that after you have pooled your personal savings, such as CDs and bank accounts, downsized your house; sold a duplex you purchased and lived in early in your job or career, you have personal savings of $200,000. This is not your total retirement income. Your retirement will also be supported by your pension and Social Security.

Withdrawing Interest. The $200,000 is a principal amount that will generate interest over time. Will you spend only the interest or will you tap the principal as well? If you spend only the interest, the principal will never diminish. Neither will it grow. If you spend the interest and some of the principal, over time, both principal and interest will decrease. If you spend part of the interest and none of the principal, both will increase. Here is a comprehensive way to look at it:

Action taken	What happens to the principal	What happens to the interest
1. Spend all the interest	1. Remains the same	1. Varies depending on the rate of interest earned
2. Spend all the interest and some principal	2. Decreases over time	2. Decreases over time
3. Spend some interest but no principal	3. Increases over time	3. Increases over time

A variable factor is the interest rate. Should interest rates increase or decrease over time, the effect on both principal and interest is impacted. In 2015, interest rates are historically low, depending on the length the principal is left on deposit. [23] Savings and money market accounts earn less than 1%, while longer term CDs yield only 2-3%.

What would $200,000 generate per year if no principal were tapped? Here are various scenarios, depending on the interest rate.

Interest Rate	Amount per year	Amount per month	Value of Principal
2%	$4000	$333	$200,000
3%	$6000	$500	$200,000
5%	$10000	$833	$200,000
7%	$14000	$1167	$200,000
10%	$20000	$1667	$200,000

Since withdrawing interest only will probably not generate enough money to live on, even with pension and Social Security, many retirees withdraw principal over time as well. This is premised on life expectancy. Do you think you are going to live 25 years after retirement? Do you want to deplete your resources near the time you die? Then you withdraw both interest and principal. At the conclusion of 25 years, you have neither principal nor interest. You are broke. You may also no longer be alive.

T. and C. think they will sell their home. Although it is not completely paid for, they believe they can net around $165,000 after closing costs and real estate commissions from their equity. With the $85,000 in personal savings and $16,500 in IRAs, they will have personal savings of $266,500 on which to live until they begin to draw Social Security, probably in two years when they both turn 62. At 4% interest in a CD, this will generate only $888 in interest per month on which to live. This

---

[23] https://www.bankofamerica.com/deposits/bank-account-interest-rates.go

is far from sufficient since they will need to rent an apartment once their home is sold. With these financial realities, they decide to stick it out at least another two years until they are eligible for Social Security and assess the financial realities of supporting a good retirement. In the meanwhile, they promise themselves to save considerably more in their remaining years in the workforce.

Withdrawing Interest and Principal. Withdrawing principal over 25 years reduces your interest and principal over time but keeps your principal withdrawal the same. This is not a bad idea if you think your needs and activities will diminish over time. Perhaps you will travel when you first retire at age 65. Fifteen years later, when you are 80, you may not want to travel at all and will have given up driving and a car, thus reducing expenses. You may have even sold your downsized home again and moved into a condominium or assisted-living center. No one, however, wants to outlive his or her savings. This is not likely to happen, however, if you plan to deplete your savings over a longer period than your life expectancy and you have the other two pools of resources, company pension and Social Security. At 65, your life expectancy is 19.3 years if a male, 21.6 years if a female. [24] Therefore, you will want to deplete your principal over 25-35 years to be safe. This source cautions that one of every four who reach 65 will live to be over 90, one of every ten will live to be over 95. [25]

Appendix 1 provides several scenarios for withdrawing interest and principal on $200,000 over 25 years at varying interest rates.

Although the depletion of principal seems like a daunting scenario, remember two things:

(1) Because of inflation, your principal will undoubtedly decline over time whether you withdraw it or not. Regardless of the inflation rate, your principal never

---

[24] https://socialsecurity.gov/planners/lifeexpectancy.html
[25] *Ibid.*

retains its original value. If you have $200,000 in savings that you never touch, it still declines in value as the years progress. This is the bad news;

(2) Because of inflation, your other two pools of retirement income, company pension and Social Security, will increase over time. Social Security is indexed to the Consumer Price Index and is adjusted upward at the beginning of each calendar year. [26] In recent years, the adjustment has been minimal (for 2015 there is no adjustment) because inflation has been almost non-existent, compared to 1980 and 1981, where the adjustment was 14.3 and 11.2, respectively. Similarly, a company pension or 401k plan, indexed indirectly to the rise and fall of market forces, such as the Dow Jones Average or NASDAQ Composite, will rise over time. This is the good news.

Finally, you will not live forever anyway and there may still be money left after your demise.

T. and L. have $200,000 in personal savings. They plan to withdraw interest only over the next twenty years. If the inflation rate is 4% for each of those years, however, the buying power of their interest as well as the $200,000 will decline. At the end of the first year, their interest and the $200,000 will only be worth 96% of what it had been. At the end of 10 years, it will be 67%. At the end of twenty years, this will only be 45%. This is the bad news.

Since their Social Security and pension payments may increase close to the rate of inflation, the combined $4000 they began to receive upon retirement will become $5920 at the end of 10 years, $8764, if the inflation rate is 4%. This is the good news.

---

[26] https://www.ssa.gov/OACT/COLA/colaseries.html

The realistic news, however, is that it will require $8764 to purchase
what they need in twenty years, not $4000. Their gain is only on paper.

Annuities. Some retirees purchase an annuity for financial security. An annuity is similar to the scenario above, where you withdraw interest and some principal over a period of time. The insurance company that sells the annuity administers it. Typically, the annuity exists for as long as you live. If you buy a 25-year annuity and live 30 more years, you win. If you die within 5 years, you lose, both life and money, depending on the stipulations in your contract. The remaining money does not necessarily become a part of your estate. In short, an annuity is a contract of support.

There are several types of annuities. If you do not have a lump sum of cash to buy an annuity and have several years to work before retirement, you purchase an annuity over a period of time through multiple payments, either monthly or annually. This is a **deferred annuity**. However, if you are close to retirement and have cash from the sale of a large asset like a house, you purchase an annuity with a single payment. This is a **lump-sum annuity**. In addition, you can put cash down and add to the amount over a period of time, which might be attractive if you have several years until retirement.

Regardless how you pay for the annuity, whether all at once or over a series of years, this is the **accumulation phase**. When you retire, which must be at age 59 1/2 or older in order to escape a 10% tax penalty (since your earnings are growing on a tax-deferred basis), you begin to draw payments from the company. This is the **withdrawal phase**.

An annuity can be contracted which provides an income stream for life or for a set period of time. If you die, there may be a guaranteed death benefit. Your heirs will receive the remainder of what you have contributed, should it not all be paid out at your demise

With most annuities, a surviving spouse may continue to receive a set percentage, such as 50%, 66 2/3% or 75% of the deceased annuitant's payment. This arrangement is coupled with corresponding reduction of the original monthly payments, depending on the contract. The higher percentage remaining for a surviving spouse, the lower the monthly payment the annuitant will receive from the outset.

Similarly, a guarantee of five or ten year's payout, regardless how long the annuitant lives, results in a corresponding reduction in monthly payments. Although this seems punitive, these reductions may be necessary when the surviving spouse has never been in the workforce or not long enough to accumulate his or her own savings. Without such arrangements, a surviving spouse would be left with no personal savings.

There are several ways to invest funds in an annuity. A **fixed annuity** promises a guaranteed rate of return for a set period of time, usually 1 to 3 years. After this, the rate is recalculated for the next 1-3 years over the period of accumulation. There is little risk. Once you begin to draw the money, the rate is similarly fixed.

By contrast, a **variable annuity** invests your accumulation in stocks or bonds, which does not guarantee a rate of return. Your original investment might be worth more or less upon retirement, depending on the market. Risk is higher but is mitigated over a series of years. This is undoubtedly a long-term plan for those in their early accumulation years. When you begin to draw income, the flow of payments may similarly vary according to stock and bond markets.

There are almost infinite variations on the types of contracts that can be written, including an equity-indexed annuity, one based on the performance of a stock index, such as the NASDAQ Composite Index or the Standard & Poor's 500 Index.

The upsides to purchasing an annuity are many. It guarantees income for life, even a set amount if you purchase a fixed annuity. There is little risk, as long as the contracting company is large and well established. Unlike many plans, there are no limits on contributions. Some plans provide bonus rates after you have been enrolled for a number of years. This increases your investment. And there are usually no initial sales charges (no load) or annual fees. All of your money accumulates from the first day. In addition, your funds are tax-deferred until you begin to draw them. Even then, you never pay taxes on your initial investment. You already have. Income taxes are only paid on what the investment has earned. Upon your death, there is no probate on remaining funds, if any, as long as you have specified beneficiaries. Your beneficiaries will have to pay income taxes as ordinary income on what remains, unlike stocks, bonds and real estate, which step up in value at your demise, resulting in no tax for heirs.

There is equally a downside to annuities. You lose some control of your money, which might be good or bad for you. There are administrative fees inherent in all contracts and transactions, such as investment management fees, account fees, and transfer fees. You can typically roll these plans over into a similar plan through a 1035 exchange.[27] As such, an annuity should only be purchased with determination that it is the right investment to guarantee retirement income.

> *If T. and C. took the $266,500 from the sale of their house and purchased a 25-year annuity at 5%, it would yield around $1500 per month for the 25-year period without any special arrangements for survivorship. At age 62, with $1550 per month in combined Social Security benefits, their monthly income would be $3050 or $36,600 per year.* [28]

---

[27] Named for Section 1035 of the Federal Tax Code, which allows one annuity to be exchanged for another annuity without income tax consequences.

[28] http://www.moneychimp.com/calculator/annuity_calculator.htm

Reverse Mortgages. Closely related to personal savings is the **reverse mortgage**.[29] This operates much like an annuity but it is not something you do in advance of retirement. You do it when you retire and it provides a flow of cash to you for years.

Since many retirees' greatest personal savings is home ownership, a finance company buys a retiree's home over a period of time, such as 30 years, paying the person monthly, just like an annuity. The retiree, who must be at least 62, remains in the house for the duration of the contract or his or her life, whichever comes first. When purchasing a home with a mortgage, you build equity and reduce debt. With a reverse mortgage, the opposite applies. You reduce equity and build debt. With each payment, equity in the house is reduced. Should he or she outlive the contract, the retiree remains in the home. Upon death, the remaining equity becomes part of the deceased's estate.

As with annuities, there are administrative costs associated with a reverse mortgage that disallow one from receiving full value of the house or to gain from the property's appreciation over time. Only the finance company gains from appreciation over time. Such a contract limits one's geographical mobility and choice of residence. Nonetheless, for some retirees, it is a solution for funding retirement with personal savings.

Although you would not make a decision on a reverse mortgage until you retire, owning your home debt-free at that time gives you this option. For readers still in the workforce, prepaying your mortgage now may enable you to own your home mortgage-free.

Carry-backs. One can sell a home and carry-back the mortgage themselves. This is like a reverse mortgage except you no longer have the house to live in. You buy a smaller house or rent. The value of the home you are selling is invested at a set interest rate, slightly higher than financial institutions are charging since the buyer does not have loan-

---

[29] http://portal.hud.gov/hudportal/HUD?src=/program_offices/housing/sfh/hecm/rmtopten

origination fees. The monthly payment is based on interest on the unpaid balance as well as a return of a portion of the principal.

As the loan repayments progress, monthly payments remain the same. Each month, the amount of interest decreases while the return of principal increases until the loan is fully paid. This is a tempting way to get cash out of your home when you retire. However, a 30-year payout (amortization) is never good for someone who is in his or her sixties. It is better to have a balloon payment due for the balance at the end of 5-7 years. What is not paid at your death becomes part of your estate. Administration of the loan repayment is best managed through an escrow company so accounting is precise. Late payments can be accompanied with a punitive fee to mitigate their occurrence. The financing arrangement must always be secured with a deed of trust as well as a promissory note so you, as the seller, are protected in case of default.

S. is single. He is retiring in the next few months and has purchased a used Class C motor home in which he plans to travel full time for the first five years of his retirement. After that, he will probably sell the motor home, if he is tired of full-timing, and rent an apartment. His modest home, which he bought thirty years ago for $30,000, is free and clear. In addition, it is now worth $275,000, a bargain for the community in which he lives.

The buyers have asked S. to carry back a promissory note, secured by a deed of trust. Since they will have to pay neither loan origination points nor mortgage insurance premiums, they are willing to pay a rate of interest higher than the market if S. will sell with a 10% down payment. S. has obtained a credit check on them and found they pay their bills. They have a respectable FICO.[30] Although he agrees to carry back the

---

[30] https://en.wikipedia.org/wiki/FICO

loan for 5 years at 5%, it will be amortized over a 30-year period. The borrowers will make payments as if it were a 30-year loan, but will pay off the remainder of the loan at the end of 5 years.

At the end of the five years, S. will receive a lump-sum payout of the balance and the buyers will need to find a new mortgage. From this carry back, S. will receive $1325 [31] per month for the first five years, most of which will be interest. At the end of the five years, he will receive a lump sum of almost $222,500. As a single person, he will owe no capital gains tax on this amount, since his gain has been less than $250,000 ($275,000-$30,000.)[32]

If your home is free and clear at retirement, the carry-back provides another option.

How much personal savings do you need? As discussed in Chapter One, it depends on the percentage (70%-130%) of pre-retirement income you want. It depends on what portion your personal savings will contribute to your total retirement funds along with pension and Social Security. There are worksheets at chapter's end to guide you through necessary calculations.

There is a simple rule, some say a myth, about how much you need to have saved for retirement. If you presently have $30,000 in take-home pay per year and anticipate you will need this much in retirement, you need to accumulate twenty-five times this amount, $750,000, for retirement. [33] But if you anticipate that Social Security benefits and a company pension will provide two-thirds of that annual amount, then you only need $10,000 per year, an accumulation of $250,000.

---

[31] http://www.amortization-calc.com

[32] http://www.investopedia.com/ask/answers/06/capitalgainhomesale.asp

[33] http://www.early-retirement.org/forums/f28/you-probably-need-25-to-30-times-your-current-salary-saved-to-retire-27061.html

The documented need for personal savings is not well supported by facts. [34] Americans have the lowest savings rate of any modern country in the world and the personal savings rate even entered negative territory in 1998. In that year, Americans spent $10.02 for every $10.00 they brought. Although the savings rate has improved, it is largely generation-based, older workers manifesting the largest pool of retirement funding. [35] Unfortunately, this is only an average and it is estimated that a third of workers have less than $1000 socked away for retirement. [36]

Pensions: The second pool of retirement income, the company pension, has been used in a generic manner throughout this text. Pensions vary a great deal from workplace to workplace, job to job, and profession to profession. Unlike personal savings that you accomplish on your own, a company pension, however named and constituted, is an obligatory plan in which you participate because it is part of the employment package and benefits. Typically, the employer contributes to the funding of the pension to some degree, sometimes matching your contribution, dollar for dollar.

In the traditional pension, the employer could be the Federal government, a state government, or even a county or municipality. Large companies with numerous employees also create pension funds. The larger the fund, the more likely it represents many types of jobs, professions and careers. A state pension might include teachers, professors, law enforcement officers, firefighters, social and welfare workers, and prison guards.

There are two types of pensions: (1) one that promises a set retirement income, a **defined-benefit plan**; and (2) one that requires a set contribution with no promise of ultimate benefits, a **defined-contribution plan**.

---

[34] http://blog.careerexplorer.net/random-thoughts/how-much-do-americans-save
[35] *Ibid*.
[36] http://www.usatoday.com/story/money/personalfinance/2014/03/18/retirement-confidence-survey-savings/6432241/

22

Defined-benefit plan: This plan assumes that employees enter the workforce and stay with the employer for most if not their entire career. The defined-benefit pension is administered by a board of directors, which determines what the benefit will be, based on each person's highest salary and years of service. Periodically, possibly each year, the board determines how much each employee must contribute to support current retirees. Each employee might contribute 2% of income one year, but 3% in another year, depending on what is required to maintain the fund and pay the current retirees. The employer often matches this contribution. When one retires, the benefit is determined by multiplying the years of service by a set percentage, such as 2% or 2.5%. The employee's highest salary while employed, possibly averaged over the last two to five years, determines the benefit.

In many pensions, the greater the years of service, the higher the percentage paid. With 10 years of service or less, the factor might be 1.5%. After 15 years, this would elevate to 2%, after 20 to 2.2%, and after 25, possibly 2.5%. Such a pension rewards loyalty and longevity. If a person does not have sufficient years of service, he or she is not vested. In the event of termination before retirement, he or she receives a lump sum of what was paid in without the employer's contribution. In most plans one is vested after five years of employment. Once you retire, your pension funds are annuitized (just as described above). The only difference is that the pension fund has purchased the annuity for you. Appendix 2 outlines typical scenarios with different percentages:

> *C. has worked for a small corporation for 27.5 years as a marketing manager. The company offers a defined-benefit pension based on the average of the five top salary years for the employee, which for C. is $64,000. For each year of service, she will receive 2.05% of the average salary. C.'s pension will provide $36,080 per year (56% of her pre-retirement salary) or $3007 per month. Social Security will provide another $1200 per month. This is almost 80% of her pre-retirement income.*

23

The Federal government supports several retirement plans. Civil Service Retirement System (CSRS) calculates retirement income based on years of service. A percentage figure is used with the average of the employee's top three years of salary. The first five years of service provide 1.5 % for each year, the next five, 1.75%, and thereafter each year contributes 2%, thus rewarding longevity. CSRS employees typically do not pay into Social Security and have no benefits there if their only employment has been government. Retirement with 25 years of service and an average salary of $50,000 would provide $23,125 annually in retirement. This calculation is shown in Appendix 3.

By contrast, an employee covered by the Federal Employees Retirement System (FERS) receives 1% for each year of his or her service unless they are at least 62 and have 20 or more years of service, in which case the multiplier is 1.1%. FERS employees may also contribute to a Thrift Savings Plan, thus blending their total retirement package between a defined-benefit and a defined-contribution plan. In addition, they pay Social Security tax and will eventually receive a benefit from that program.

With an average salary of $50,000, the benefit with FERS for 25 years of service would be $13,750, as seen in Appendix 4

Although the above figures do not provide 70% or 100% or 130% of pre-retirement income, personal savings and Social Security (with the exception of CSRS) elevate the final retirement income figure. Without doubt, public pensions are an excellent system for employees in education, public safety and welfare. Many pensions include a cost-of-living adjustment (COLA), which raises the benefit periodically. There is some belief that the largesse of these pension plans compensates for the traditionally low salaries paid to public servants. These pensions have come under public scrutiny and may be changed over the next generation. Many feel this arrangement is doomed. [37] Between 1985 and

---

[37] https://www.ssa.gov/policy/docs/ssb/v69n3/v69n3p1.html

2011, defined benefit pension plans declined 77%, in both public and private sectors.[38] Although 90% of Fortune 100 companies offered a defined benefit pension in 1998, by 2012, it was 30%. [39] In the private sector , the alleged generosity of this type of pension has been replaced with the defined-contribution plans.

Defined-contribution plan: Although an employee contributes a set amount, whether percentage or dollar figure, the ultimate payout at retirement is not guaranteed. Funds are invested in the stock market, which has a variable rate of return.   The ultimate return cannot be defined.   The average rate of return per year on the stock market has been between 10-12%, [40] but there is no guarantee it will do better or worse in the future. [41] An employee may find his or her contributions outpace the 2% guaranteed by a defined-benefit plan.   In down market cycles, the investments might do worse.   Although the employer typically matches these funds, the ultimate payout is not indexed to one's pre-retirement salary, only to what is contributed and matched.

Since many jobs and careers necessitate frequent moves, defined-benefit pensions are becoming rare and defined-contribution plans more common.   Unless a person works for the Federal government, whose pensions are similar from location to location, or the military, such pensions, if administered by a state, county or municipality, are terminated when the person leaves the area for another position.   At this willful termination, the employee withdraws his or her contributions (but usually not the matching funds of the employer) and moves on to the next entity.   The funds could then be spent or re-invested, with potential income tax consequences.   With a series of moves throughout one's employment lifetime, the retirement funds are minimal because the matching funds of the employers have been left behind.   Most entities allow departing employee , if vested,[42] to keep funds in the pension and draw on them eventually when they retire.   But since the

---

[38] http://www.limra.com/uploadedFiles/limracom/Posts/PR/_Media/PDFs/Disappearing-DB-Pension-Plan.pdf

[39] *Ibid*.

[40] http://www.ehow.com/info_7848194_average-stock-market-rate-return.html

[41] Free Financial Advice, 1384 Florida Street, San Francisco, CA 94110

[42] http://money.cnn.com/retirement/guide/pensions_pensions.moneymag/index4.htm

benefit will be determined on the salary at termination, the ultimate benefit, twenty or thirty years hence, could be minimal.

To mitigate this situation, portable pension plans were developed that systemically do the same thing. These are 401ks, 403bs, 457s, SEPs and IRAs. These are usually defined-contribution pensions.

Portable Pensions. The **401k plan**[43] is named for a section (401k) of the Internal Revenue Code of 1978, [44] which allows an employee of a corporation to set up a defined contribution savings plan. Money is contributed before income taxes are paid, reducing the employee's annual gross income. Since income tax is ultimately paid upon retirement, a 401k is tax deferred. In addition, the employer, who administers the plan, may contribute to the plan, sometimes matching the employee's contribution dollar-for-dollar. Businesses and large corporations prefer this type of pension since costs of implementing and supporting are lower than a defined benefit plan. Whatever each person's account grows to be upon retirement determines the ultimate benefit.

Similarly, the **403b plan** is for employees in non-profit organizations whereas the **457 plan** covers employees of municipal, county and state governments. Since there is a large penalty for withdrawing money before retirement, 10%, plus responsibility for the income taxes, this is not like a personal savings account. [45] It is money earmarked for retirement.

---

[43] https://www.irs.gov/Retirement-Plans/401(k)-Resource-Guide
[44] https://en.wikipedia.org/wiki/Revenue_Act_of_1978
[45] The 10% penalty does not apply to 457 plans, regardless of when the money is withdrawn. (Taxes do apply.) If the funds are rolled over to an IRA, however, withdrawal would trigger the penalty before age 59 1/2.

There is a limit on how much a worker may contribute to these plans. For 2015 and 2016, it is $18,000. In addition, employees over age 50 can contribute an additional $6000 as "catch-up". [46]

This are remarkable plans and they encourage retirement savings because tax is deferred on what is saved until you draw on it (you must be 59 1/2). If the stock market is good, funds invested in equities will grow. When you eventually pay tax on both the principal (what you paid in) plus the gain (what has grown), you may be in a lower income tax bracket. The 10% penalty for early withdrawal is a strong deterrent from using funds to pay for a new roof on your house, buy a new car or travel to Tahiti.

Nonetheless, there are certain conditions that allow you to draw the money without penalty (but still with tax), such as catastrophic illness or disability, purchase of a first home, college expenses, or death. You can borrow against this money in the short-term as well without destroying your retirement account. And most compelling, these plans may be converted (termed a "rollover") to other similar and qualified plans should you change employment. The 401k and its cousins are truly portable pensions.

Do workers participate in these plans if they are available at their place of employment? Fifty-two million American workers had this type of plan in 2012, [47] which is only 36% of the workforce. Of those who do, the average account has a value of $77,300.[48]

The average participant saves about 6% of their salary in these plans. [49] And 76% of workers who are eligible to participate do. [50] But only 58% of employers provide some match to contributions, typically 50 cents on the dollar, up to the first 6% contributed by

[46] http://www.401kirarollover.com/401k-Plans-Contribution-Limits-Salary-Deferral-Pre-Tax.html
[47] https://www.ici.org/policy/retirement/plan/401k/faqs_401k
[48] http://www.iravs401kcentral.com/have-an-average-401k-balance/
[49] http://www.cbsnews.com/news/five-401k-mistakes-to-avoid/
[50] http://www.ebri.org/surveys/rcs/1997/index.cfm?fa=401k

the employee. [51] In the past two decades, fewer companies have offered a 401k plan. Of those who do, the contribution rate has been reduced from the generosity of earlier years.

> *L. has had five positions since she entered the workforce twenty years ago. Since each position was with a different company, each of which had a 401k plan, she simply rolled-over her funds to the new 401k plan of each firm as she moved up the career ladder. Although she is only 42 years old and anticipates working until she is 62 and can draw Social Security, her accumulation of wealth from the 401k plan is currently $195,500. She knows it will more than double in the remaining twenty years she will have in the workforce. When she retires, she will roll everything into an Individual Retirement Account and then withdraw whatever is required and that she needs to live on.   Since the 401k contributions occurred before she paid income tax on the earnings, she will pay tax as she withdraws.*

A **SEP (Simplified Employer Pension Plan)** is a similar plan for self employed (independent contractors) and small business owners.   If a person is self-employed, he or she can contribute $18,000 or 25% of their compensation into a SEP as a tax-deductible expense. [52] The employer may also fund employees' SEP (employees do not contribute) up to 25% of each worker's annual salary ($53,000 maximum). This is tax deductible for the business as an operating expense.

The **Simple IRA** is similar to the SEP. It is specifically for companies which have 100 or fewer employees. It does not require a third party administrator and is easier to establish and to maintain. Employees may contribute up to $12,500 while the employer may contribute up to the employee's salary reduction amount. The match is limited, however,

---

[51] http://www.benefitspro.com/2013/05/02/fewer-employers-match-401k-contributions
[52] https://www.irs.gov/Retirement-Plans/Plan-Participant,-Employee/SEP-Contribution-Limits-including-grandfathered-SARSEPs

to 3% of the employee's salary, which would require a salary of $415,557 for the maximum match. [53]

Finally, the **IRA (Individual Retirement Account)** is the most portable of all pension plans. Contributions are tax deductible as long as the worker has earned income. Although there is a limit on the contribution, depending on your income range, you can contribute $5500 if you are under age 50, or $6500 if 50 or older in 2015. [54] Older workers are provided with some "catch up" as well. When you draw income from the IRA, which cannot occur before age 59 1/2 without penalty, you pay taxes on everything you withdraw, since the original principal gave you a break on income taxes for the years contributed. Since both principal and interest are tax-deferred, you pay taxes on everything. But as with other plans, you may be in a lower tax bracket by the time you retire.

A **Roth IRA** [55] is a recent variation on the traditional IRA. Named for Senator William V. Roth, Jr., it was part of the Taxpayer Relief Act of 1997. Although it does not allow you to deduct contributions on your current income tax return, all earnings are tax-free when you withdraw them. The contribution limitations are the same as for the regular IRA and you are limited by income level.

All of the portable pensions require you to begin withdrawing tax-deferred income when you reach your early 70s, based on your life expectancy. [56] The federal government provides great incentives to save on a tax-deferred basis, but, at some point, the tax must be paid. [57] If you die and tax deferred accounts still exist, your estate eventually pays taxes when the money is withdrawn.

---

[53] https://www.americanfunds.com/individual/products/simple-ira.html?k_clickid=785c46ad-4f24-4b72-98af-718bb2be54e5&cid=ps_msn_34632
[54] https://investor.vanguard.com/ira/ira-contribution-limits?WT.srch=1
[55] http://www.rothira.com
[56] https://personal.vanguard.com/us/insights/retirement/estimate-your-rmd-tool
[57] https://www.irs.gov/Retirement-Plans/Plan-Participant,-Employee/Retirement-Topics-Required-Minimum-Distributions-(RMDs)

Saving for retirement is a compelling part of our country's social policy. Incentives are high for employees to provide part of their retirement income. We are not entitled to a grand retirement because we have reached a retirement age, but, rather, because we have exercised prudence and restraint in saving for the future consistently for a long period of time, and, with government approval. If you want to retire with ample means, these programs allow it.

Social Security: Social Security is **FICA** (Federal Insurance Contributions Act), the obligatory pool, whether you are self-employed or work for someone else. It was enacted in 1935 under Franklin Delano Roosevelt's administration.[58] Although some federal, state and municipal pension plans do not require employees to contribute to Social Security, these are the only workers who do not pay into the fund. (Nor will they reap its rewards at retirement!) All other employees pay this tax with each paycheck at the rate of 6.2% to a cap of $118,000 for 2015. The employer matches this tax with an identical 6.2%.[59]

There has always been skepticism about Social Security. Its costs and benefits have changed over time, but it will probably not go away. It is a social contract endowed by the Federal government that has existed for eighty years. It is not a savings plan and it is not a pension; rather, Social Security is a tax for current employees and an entitlement for retirees. It provides 39% of the income of the elderly.[60] Unlike a savings plan and pension, the funds you pay in do not go into a separate account with your name on it. They go into the general fund. Social Security is a "pay-as-you-go" plan. Current workers pay for present retirees. Future workers will in turn pay when these workers reach retirement age. In 1950, 16 workers supported each recipient while only 2.8

---

[58] http://www.u-s-history.com/pages/h1609.html
[59] https://www.ssa.gov/OACT/COLA/cbb.html
[60] https://www.ssa.gov/news/press/basicfact.html

workers support each presently.[61] In twenty years, this will drop to only 2.1 workers per recipient, which has created numerous doubts about the solvency of the system. [62]

Social Security has been refined and reformated over time to adjust to changing demographics. Baby Boomers retiring in large number have stressed the system, as it would any social program, but it will endure. Benefits may diminish and required contributions (tax) may increase. Retirement ages for full benefits have already moved from 65 (those born in 1937 and earlier) to 66 (for those born 1943-1954) to 67 (those born 1960 or later.) [63] Workers in the notch years between have had their retirement age lengthened correspondingly as well.

When the full retirement age for Social Security was 65 (retiree was born in 1937 or earlier), applying for benefits at 62 resulted in payments 20% less than those received at 65. As the retirement age moves to 67 (phased in for workers born 1938 or later), applying for benefits at 62 will ultimately result in payments 30% less than those received at 67. An example is provided in Appendix 5.

R, was born in 1936. He waited until he was 65 to begin drawing Social Security in 2001 and received $1400 per month in benefits at that time. Had he elected to begin Social Security benefits at age 62, he would have received $1120 per month. By contrast, his daughter, who was born in 1954, would have to wait until she was 66 to receive the $1400 monthly check, if her earning history were the same as his. If she were to elect to begin Social Security at age 62, her monthly benefit would be $1050.

_____

[61] *Ibid*

[62] Social Security Online *www.socialsecurity.gov*

[63] https://www.socialsecurity.gov/planners/retire/agereduction.html

This will undoubtedly create strong motivation for workers to wait until 67 or later to retire, if they are healthy. You need 5% less income for each year you work beyond normal retirement age because there is a benefit increase in Social Security for each year. This is particularly important for those who did not begin personal savings and pension funds at an early age. Even at age 50, it is hard to do "catch up".

What about spouses covered under Social Security? If they have had their own job and career, they receive their own benefits. If they have not worked or if earnings over the work lifetime are minimal, they receive half of the main recipient's benefits. If there is a question about which applies, the higher benefit always does. Benefits paid before full retirement age, as described above, are permanently reduced pro rata.

Social Security was never intended to be a total retirement plan. In 1990 Social Security replaced 43% of the pre-retirement income of a typical employee. It has dropped to 39%, 25 years later in 2015. Among married couples, 22% depend on Social Security for 90% or more of their income. For unmarried persons, it is 47%.[64]

An employee may request a projection of benefits from the Social Security Administration at any time.[65] After 62, the Social Security office sends an annual report on your birthdate. The Social Security administration website allows you to estimate your benefits[66] to facilitate retirement planning.

Summary. Before you move on, complete this chart:

Pre-retirement income (per year)	$ **
Percentage I need of pre-retirement income to retire (70-130%)	%
What my personal savings will earn (per year)	$

---

[64] https://www.ssa.gov/news/press/basicfact.html
[65] https://www.ssa.gov/myaccount/
[66] http://www.ssa.gov/onlineservices/

What my pension will earn (per year)	$
What I will receive from Social Security (per year)	$
My total retirement income (per year)	$ *
Percentage my retirement income will be of my pre-retirement income (divide * by **)	%

If you have made it through this chapter and can identify the three pools of retirement funding and how you will make these sufficient for your needs, you are ready to proceed to the next chapters.

Chapter Three

Money for Retirement: What are the financial realities of retirement?

In Chapter Two, it was determined what is needed to sustain the lifestyle you want. In this chapter, the detail of managing those funds is considered.

Fixed Income. The first myth to dispel is "fixed income". Many retirees spew forth this label as a self-fulfilling prophecy or reason for entitlement. Your income will not be fixed in retirement. It will vary every year. Social Security benefits ratchet up each new year based on the CPI (Consumer Price Index), adjusted to reflect products and services retirees do or do not buy. In January 2014, the increase was 1.5%; January 2015, 1.7%. When inflation is higher, the increase is greater.   For 2016, there is no adjustment because inflation was non-existent. [67]

If you have variable annuities and 401ks based on stock and bond funds, income will be variable. Income in retirement may be less fixed than it was during your working years. There is probably no such thing as fixed income, whether one is working or retired. The label is inappropriate. It suggests deprivation or entitlement.   When you do retire, your flow of funds will grow over time if you invest wisely.   Nothing is fixed in life, particularly neither your pre- nor post-retirement income.

J. and R. love to say they live on a "fixed income" and cannot afford it whenever their children or grandchildren ask them to fly out for a visit. Their son-in-law, however, pointed out that they enjoyed a 1.7% cost of living adjustment on their Social Security at the beginning of 2015 as well as a 3.5% raise on Ruth's pension in mid-2014. They reinvested a CD, which had earned 1.5% in the last two years, at 2.0 % for 18 months. "Doesn't look fixed to me", said their son-in-law. "Wish my

---

[67] https://www.ssa.gov/news/cola/automatic-cola.htm

salary would jump that much in a year!" They still declined to make the trip.

Income Tax. A financial reality for retirees is: "But I still have to pay income taxes!" If there is income, there will be income tax. The only exception is when principal is returned. In a savings account, money was saved after taxes were paid. This money will not be taxed but interest earned will be. The bank or financial institution provides a 1099-I form at the end of each year and tax is due on the interest. What may change in retirement is that you might be in a lower tax bracket and will owe less.

Pension plans, whether federal, state, municipal, corporate, or portable will similarly require payment of income tax. Since this money is frequently contributed before taxes, income tax was deferred to a later time. The federal and state governments require tax on it. This is typically withheld in the monthly payment, much like it was before retirement. You may need to re-evaluate and adjust withholding rates. It is better to err on the side of having too much withheld your first year of retirement. In subsequent years, you can assess how this affects your tax return and change the allocation. Many retirees pay estimates to prevent a gigantic tax liability the first year of retirement.

Even the third prong of retirement funds, Social Security, may be taxable. If these benefits were your only income, you would not pay income taxes. You would also not be living very well. Income taxes on Social Security benefits are a means test. If you are better off, you pay some income tax.

The calculation to determine tax on benefits depends on filing status. If you file your tax return jointly, $32,000 is presently the magic (base amount) number ($25,000 if you are single). If half of your Social Security benefits plus all other income, including tax-exempt interest (Roth IRA) and tax-deferred pension, exceed this base amount, you pay income tax on half of your Social Security benefit. However, the tax can be ratcheted up another notch. If half of your benefits plus your other income exceeded $44,000 ($34,000 if you are single), 85% of the benefits are taxable. [68]

These amounts will undoubtedly change before you retire, but there is no free lunch. The reward for thrift and frugality is a better life style, not lower income taxes. You can take comfort in realizing that your colleagues who did not save for retirement do not pay taxes on their Social Security benefits. They probably do not have enough income.

K. was 66 years old in 2015. She is widowed and receives $825 from her husband's pension fund, all of which was contributed before taxes. She also receives some interest income from their collective savings of $25,000, which is in a bank CD at 2%. It earns $500 per year. Her Social Security payments are $1208 per month ($14,500 per year). Although she owed $146 in income taxes for 2015, none of her Social Security benefits were taxed.

Her cousin of the same age, by contrast, has a pension, which provides $54,000 a year, also contributed before taxes. She received $13,500 in 2015 in interest income. Her Social Security benefits were also $14,500 for the year. As a result of her higher income, she was taxed on 85% of this amount, $12,325. Her Federal tax bill for 2015 was $11,184. Fortunately, she made quarterly estimated tax payments and avoided any penalty.

K., who paid very little tax, has $2075 net per month to live on. Her cousin, who paid substantial tax, has $5900 net per month.

---

[68] https://ssa.gov/planners/taxes.html

Budgeting: If you presently do not track income and expenses, it is time to begin. Although you may receive a paycheck once a week or every two weeks, most retirement income comes monthly. Convert your budget from weekly to monthly and begin to hold back pools of money (accrual accounting) to meet needs in a timely fashion. This way, your budget will carry you through to retirement.

Why is a budget important? There is no better way to be fiscally accountable and monitor what you spend versus what you bring in. Consider these ideas to make budgeting efficient and help you save for retirement. Here is a practical means to budget without letting the process inhibit your life.

First, list income flows

- Personal Savings
- Pension
- Social Security

Then, list expenses

- Personal allowance (1st partner)
- Personal allowance (2nd partner)
- Auto Insurance
- Auto License
- Donations
- Entertainment
- Gasoline
- Gifts
- Groceries
- Health Insurance
- House Insurance
- Income Tax

- Long Term Health Insurance
- Medicine
- Miscellaneous
- Mortgage Payments
- Periodicals and Newspapers
- Property Tax
- Savings
- Utilities
- Vacation and Travel

If you have never budgeted, begin with the money you have in your checking account. Assume it is a healthy amount, $5000. Allocate* it to the categories listed above in a realistic manner. This represents start up funds for your budget.

Budget Item	Allocation from Pool ($5000)*
Allowance (1st partner)	
Allowance (2nd partner)	
Auto Insurance	$300
Auto License	
Donations	$400
Entertainment	
Gasoline	
Gifts	
Groceries	
Health Insurance	$500
House Insurance	$200

House Repairs	$50
Income Tax	
Long Term Health Insurance	$500
Medicine	$100
Miscellaneous	
Mortgage Payments	$2000
Periodicals and Newspapers	$50
Property Tax	$500
Savings	$200
Utilities	$100
Vacation and Travel	$100
Totals	**$5000**

Next, determine actual expenses. If property taxes are due once a year, accumulate that much money in the property tax fund in advance. If property taxes are $2400 per year, accrue $200 each month in the year prior to the due date. The same is true for all annual fees, such as long term health insurance, if you have it, auto insurance and licenses. Begin to allocate at least 10-15% of your after-tax income to savings. If you do not, when you retire, you will not have personal savings. The first year of a budget is the toughest if you do not have an initial pool of money.

Thereafter, as income flows in monthly, allocate each line item its fair share. If there is $4000 after-taxes each month, here is a possible allocation.** Each month include a column of Accumulated Funds to see how much you have in each account.

Budget Item	Allocation from Pool ($5000)*	Month 1** Allocation	Month 1 Accumulation
Personal allowance 1		$120	$120
Personal Allowance 2		$120	$120
Auto Insurance	$300	$75	$375
Auto License		$30	$30
Donations	$400	$300	$700
Entertainment		$100	$100
Gasoline		$60	$60
Gifts		$40	$40
Groceries		$400	$400
Health Insurance	$500	$135	$635
House Insurance	$200	$100	$300
House Repairs	$50	$75	$125
Income Tax		$150	$150
Long Term Health Insurance	$500	$100	$600
Medicine	$100	$50	$150
Miscellaneous		$100	$100
Mortgage	$2000	$1100	$3100
Periodicals and Papers	$50	$25	$75

Property Tax	$500	$200	$700
Savings		$400	$400
Utilities	$300	$220	$520
Vacation and Travel	$100	$100	$200
Totals	$5000	$4000	$9000***

As you live through the month, there are several categories that will be tapped and even depleted. You use grocery money and gasoline for basic living. Electricity and water bills (utilities) are paid. But funds that are paid once or twice a year are left to accumulate until the money is due.

Here is what will happen in your second month's allocation. The total of the most recent month's accumulation *** is what you should have in your bank account. It is okay to go into a deficit on any one category as long as the deficit is relieved by the next month. It is okay to withdraw funds from another account (except savings) that seems "large" to support a different account as long as you do not deplete funds for a payment that might be coming up. Although it is all your money, the budget allows you to allocate, track funds and anticipate needed expenditures. It prevents money from slipping between your fingers.

N. and H. are just beginning married life. He had always spent whatever he wanted whereas she monitored income and expenses. N. always knew what bills were due, particularly those which occurred only quarterly or annually. H. just let them occur and then scrambled to come up with the cash to pay. N. began to push H. to establish a budget soon after they were married so they could save the down payment for a house as well as for retirement. He balked and said: "As long as there is money in the checking account, we're not over budget." But with her insistence, they agreed to set up a tentative budget and try it for 6 months. By that time, H. was a true believer, particularly when he saw how accruing funds for non-monthly payments worked and as they saw their down payment and retirement pools grow. In addition, they were earning interest on accumulations of cash by transferring them from the checking account to short-term CDs.

There is a personal allowance for both members of the marriage or partnership. It provides an amount that can be spent with neither accountability nor competition. In all relationships, there should be money, which is allocated without personal responsibility to the other partner. If one wants to save for an exotic trip or a set of golf clubs, so be it. If one wishes to purchase a gift for the other, it can be done without revealing when and how much.

Financial issues are a leading cause of problems in a marriage and 45% of all divorces are due to financial disagreements. [69] Although the reasons for divorce are never singular, the difference in attitude towards money contributes. It is particularly sad when this occurs after a couple has retired. Both partners in a relationship, whether retired or not, have to commit to a budget and be equally accountable to the financial goals of the union. For this reason, the "mad" money in the form of a personal allowance is a safety value for the otherwise rigidity of the system.

Appendix 6 presents a scenario of what happens in the second month, as you draw expenditures out of line items in Month 1 and add your allocations for Month 2.

This process can continue through month 3 and on throughout a year or several years as seen in Appendix 7. With this accounting, you know what you have in your checking account and how it is going to be used. It allows accrual for big expenses that come quarterly (taxes), semi-annually or annually (taxes and insurance). Most importantly it provides a slot for personal savings for retirement.

---

[69] http://www.examiner.com/article/finances-remain-leading-cause-of-divorce

There are many software programs that track income and expenses similarly, but it can be accomplished without a computer, using a spreadsheet or doing the arithmetic on a hand calculator. Although programs are convenient, budgeting does not require technology; it requires implementation and commitment.

A budget should not be sealed in stone. After six months or a year, it may be necessary to adjust line items to reflect actual need and allocate accordingly. You do not want to be short in any one account, at least not for more than a month. Similarly, there is no justice in allowing line items to accumulate when there is little likelihood you will be using those funds. Take the excess in any one account and transfer it to Savings. This way, your savings will grow more than anticipated.

In the years before retirement, continue to adjust your budget as needed, particularly with expenses that vary over time, such as groceries, taxes and utilities. Allocate most of your raises and COLAs to Savings. Should you pay off credit card debt or an automobile lease or loan, continue to budget for those expenses but place the accumulation in Savings. If you have several years before you retire, your Savings account could accumulate a considerable amount, given that you continually move the amount in a money market account or CD. You could use the monthly amount to pay into a deferred annuity. Forget the money and never use it for gifts or car down payments. It is money only for retirement, not discretionary spending.

Consolidation of Assets. Much like your dwelling, finances need to be downsized before you retire. Your assets should be consolidated into a manageable and clearly identified bundle. If you have several bank accounts in several places, put them all in one bank in fewer accounts. Every major bank provides checking, savings, CDs and money market accounts. It is a matter of choosing the best bank for you, based on their availability in several states, should you travel, as well as services such as online banking so you can monitor your accounts.

All income should be deposited directly into a working checking account, including Social Security, pension and 401k payments. This prevents the "float" that comes from normal mail service. You have the money in your account on the day the agency pays it.

Your house deed and car titles should all be filed in one place, too, preferably a home safe or bank safe deposit box. Be certain location and key are readily available. The same is true of life insurance policies and notes receivables, should you have any. Marriage (and divorce) papers should be in the same file, even birth and baptismal certificates. You are providing a financial story of your life that someone may need to complete upon your demise. Outline the plot simply and clearly. Credit card numbers, property and income tax files, wills and trusts should be part of this file.

An added component of this financial outline must include a spreadsheet of your assets and liabilities, giving a fair estimate of each asset's value at the time the spreadsheet is completed. This provides a snapshot of your estate's value to an executor. For you, it is a tracking document that can be updated periodically, preferably at the beginning of each year now and even into your retirement years. For your heirs, it will ultimately be the Rosetta stone. There is a suggested format in Appendix 8.

> *R. and M. always thought they had so little that there was no need to worry about their assets. When their three children insisted they list what they owned and what they owed, they were surprised it was so extensive.*

Item	Value	Equity	Debt
House	$162,000	$92,500	$69500
Auto 1	$15,000	$12,000	$3,000
Auto 2	$8,000	$7,000	$1,000
R.'s IRA	$22,200	$22,200	

Personal Savings	*$12,000*	*$12,000*	
Credit Card Debt			*$1,350*
Total	*$219200*	*$145,700*	*$74850*

Their son, a business major at the state university, counseled them to pay off their credit card and car loan debts as soon as possible, then to make extra payments on their mortgage so they could be debt free by the time they turned 62.

Wills and Trusts. Although you have delineated your assets and liabilities, how will these will survive you? If you were a clever retiree, you would plan to consume your last asset, without debt, on the day you die. No one is so fortunate and such a practice would put lots of estate planners and administrators out of work. It is likely you will leave some assets, maybe even substantial, to someone. If you have specific people whom you want to receive what is over, delineate it in a will or a trust. If you do not, the government of the state in which you die will do it for you, following statute law for their jurisdiction. It is better to organize your estate for final disposition long before you retire.

A **will** is a written document that specifies how your assets will be disposed of following your death. It does not need to be written by an attorney, but that is certainly the best way to have it done. Although many states accept a hand written will that is not witnessed (holograph), a bit of money saved now can result in great expense and hardship after your death, even when directions are clear.

A **trust** is a written document that accompanies a will that is more specific and private than a will, not only specifying to whom assets will be left, but how and when. The correct name for a living trust is a **revocable inter vivos trust**. You control the trust and can even change it as long as you live. A living trust allows assets to be distributed

45

without probate, a process of going to the courts to determine ownership. Probate can be lengthy and costly. Trust assets pass immediately upon your death since all assets are titled into the trust and managed by you, the trustee or settlor, until your death.

Married couples use an **AB trust** or **marital life trust**. Both persons (co-trustees) put their assets in the trust, but when the first dies, the trust can no longer be altered. The deceased spouse's assets pass to his or her heirs. The surviving spouse has the legal right to use and withdraw from the trust as long as he or she lives. Typically, the first spouse who dies has specified his or her mate as the heir anyway. When the second spouse dies, the trust assets then pass to other heirs, whether children, relatives or charitable organizations.

Wills and trusts cost to establish, but the $2000-$4000 invested upfront in these legal documents is worth the cost. If your assets at death are less than $50,000, you probably do not need the trust, just the will. Most states do not probate if the estate is less than $50,000.

M. and D. set up an AB trust when they were in their early fifties. All of their assets had to be re-titled into the trust, including their two houses, autos, life insurance policies, portfolios, retirement and bank accounts. The attorney provided forms for them to contact each agency and they were able to do much of the re-titling work themselves, saving on legal fees. Each new asset purchase or account must now be opened in the name of the trust to ensure its inclusion. When they both die, years from now hopefully, the remaining assets of the trust will pass to their heirs and designees without probate. At that point, the trust will dissolve.

Insurances: Health and Long-Term Care. None of these grand schemes is important if you do not maintain health in retirement. Health care requires attention by health providers as well as necessary prescription drugs to keep you healthy as you age. This requires health insurance.

Health Care. If you are 65 when you retire, you are automatically enrolled in Medicare. Medicare has four parts: A, B, C and D. [70] Part A is free and covers hospital stays, skilled nursing care at a facility, limited home health care and hospice care. Part B, medical insurance, is elective with a premium deducted from your Social Security benefits ($104.90 monthly in 2015, $121.80 in 2016). This is true only if your income is less than $170,000 for a married couple, $85,000 for a single person. [71] Since Medicare is means tested, there are higher rates for greater incomes. The graduated schedule of cost is shown in Appendix 9. Part C is an Advantage Plan, where a private insurance company provides Medicare benefits. Part D is outpatient prescription drug coverage.

Medicare A and B cover doctors' fees and services and outpatient hospital services. Employees pay 1.45% of their wages into Medicare, which is matched by the employer on all income. There is no cap on this tax as there is with Social Security.

Medicare Part D was instituted in 2006 and provides help for prescription costs. [72] You must have Medicare Part A and/or Part B. Numerous sponsors, each of whom has contracted with pharmaceutical companies, provide this service. It is a marketplace, where an enrollee chooses which plan is available in his or her area. Premium can be as low as $15 a month to as much as $165.40. [73] Like Medicare B, Medicare D is means tested, with an added charge depending on a retiree's income.[74]

---

[70]

http://www.medicareinteractive.org/page2.php?topic=counselor&page=script&script_id=214

[71] https://www.medicare.gov/your-medicare-costs/costs-at-a-glance/costs-at-glance.html#collapse-4809

[72] https://en.wikipedia.org/wiki/Medicare_Part_D

[73] http://kff.org/medicare/issue-brief/medicare-part-d-prescription-drug-plans-the-marketplace-in-2013-and-key-trends-2006-2013/

[74] https://www.medicare.gov/part-d/costs/premiums/drug-plan-premiums.html

Premium amounts are different in some states, specifically Alaska and Hawaii.[75] Even for those enrolled in state pharmacy assistance programs and personal health care plans, there could be additional savings on prescribed medications.

Medicare C is an Advantage program, which covers all that A and B do, plus prescription benefits of D. Medicare C can be an HMO or PPO and is regionally based. There are varying requirements and restrictions for Part C, including co-payments, visits to specialists and drug coverage. Medicare C does eliminate the need to have "gap" insurance, to cover what Medicare A and B do not allow.[76]

Much like Social Security, Medicare was never intended to be a complete system for retirees. Just as you need personal savings and a pension to retire comfortably, you need "gap" health insurance to cover what entitlement programs do not. This is your personal health care plan, which becomes a secondary provider once you are enrolled in Medicare Parts A and B. Since there are annual deductibles to Medicare, the gap insurance will generally pay the difference between what your health needs require and what Medicare will pay, unless you are enrolled in Medicare C.

Under Medicare Part A, in 2016, there is a $1266 deductible for the first hospital stay. There is no additional fee for a stay of 1-60 days, but $322 per day for days 61-90 and $644 per day for days 91-150 (Lifetime Reserve Days). After 150 days, you pay all costs. Skilled nursing care requires payment of $0 for days 1-20, $157.50 per day for days 21-100 for each benefit period and all costs after 100 days. [77] Part B has a $166 deductible per year and thereafter 20% for all approved services.

If you have surgery, this is what would happen. If your surgeon (Part B) charged $20,000, first you pay the $166 deductible, leaving a bill of $19,834. Medicare would pay $15,867.2 of that (80%), leaving a mere $3966.80 to fund on your own (including the

---

[75] Medicare. *http://www.medicare.gov/*

[76] https://medicare.com/medicare-advantage/medicare-part-c/
[77] https://www.medicare.gov/coverage/skilled-nursing-facility-care.html

$166). [78] The only good news, if there is any, is that you would not have to pay the $166 again in the same calendar year. If your hospital stay were 5 days, you would pay another $1266 (Part A). You need "gap" insurance.

The cost of "gap" insurance can be astronomical for retirees, particularly if there were only one wage earner in a marriage. Fortunately, many companies allow employees to carry over group health coverage into retirement, usually for a higher premium, but, nonetheless, without having to qualify. This is a boon for any person contemplating retirement. Because the company continues to finance some of your health coverage, it is an extension of a retirement package.

Medical insurance is a consideration for a mid-career person who is thinking about changing jobs. What does the present employer provide for retirees? What would a new company provide? Although this might not apply to self-employed persons or those retiring from a small company, it is often true for large corporations and public entities, such as the Federal government and state or municipal retirement systems. Large entities have much more leverage in purchasing group insurance from a supplier because of their large number of employees.

If one is forced to purchase gap insurance without corporate sponsorship, the choices are not as bright and undoubtedly more expensive. It would be well to look for a reliable HMO (Health Maintenance Organization) or PPO (Preferred Provider Organization) to find less expensive premiums. If you are healthy, a larger deductible is appropriate, since this usually drives down the annual premium.

In 2010, the Affordable Care Act (Obamacare) was rolled out with great celebration as well as heightened political debate. The key provisions include a Patient's Bill of Rights, to put consumers in control of their medical treatments, including the right to appeal as well as an end to arbitrary cancellation of coverage. Pre-existing conditions can no

---

[78] https://www.medicare.gov/your-medicare-costs/part-b-costs/part-b-costs.html

longer be a denial for coverage. [79] The law has proven to be convoluted but was a necessary step to provide coverage for a larger group of Americans, including young adults. Its future may be uncertain, but some type of national medical coverage will exist. Although Obamacare may be modified in the future, it is unlikely it will be totally unraveled.

The healthcare outlook in America in terms of new medications, treatments and research, is phenomenal. Unfortunately, because the cost is high, the financial outlook is correspondingly uncertain. We are creating treatments that solve age-old problems that no one can afford. The only thing to count on, whether retired or not, is increased cost and reduced benefits while enjoying these breakthroughs. As a country, it appears we can neither afford a national healthcare system nor ignore the consequences of not having one. This may not change in the near future because there is no quick fix.

Long-term Nursing Care. With increased life expectancy, the later years of retirement may be spent in a care facility, whether temporarily or until death. This is a reality of living longer. At least 70% of people over 65 will need nursing care at some time. [80] Will Medicare cover these extended stays in skilled nursing facilities? Not forever. As described above, there is a hefty fee of $157.50 per day from the 21st to 100th day for each benefit period. However, if you had to remain long-term in a nursing home, Medicare would lapse on day 101. With nursing home fees running from $250-300 a day, [81] one's personal savings could soon be consumed. The alternative is long-term nursing care insurance. This is a costly endeavor but lowering the benefit can reduce premiums. A policy that pays as long as you remain in a nursing home is the most expensive. One that guarantees four years is less costly. Many people do not remain in a nursing home that long. The average stay is 835 days. [82] Although some eventually return home, many die before the four years have passed.

---

[79] http://www.hhs.gov/healthcare/about-the-law/index.html
[80] https://www.lifehappens.org/blog/startling-facts-about-long-term-care/
[81] https://www.genworth.com/corporate/about-genworth/industry-expertise/cost-of-care.html
[82] *Ibid*., https://www.lifehappens.org/

J. and S. both had grandparents who were moved into a nursing facility in their later years, dying within two years. Since they are now young, they can purchase a long-term nursing policy for indefinite stay for $950 per year each. A less expensive alternative is to limit the stay to four years or less, adding a home-care rider on the policy for the same amount of time. This is somewhat less expensive at $625 a year. With their family history they realize they may need long-term care in their senior years. The longer they wait to purchase a policy, the more it will cost. They opt for the $625 a year premium.

A four-year cap might be sufficient. It depends on family history and genetics as well as the illness that requires nursing care. Long-term care policies should be purchased in one's early years, since the older you are, the higher the premium. Nonetheless, there is nothing more important for preserving an estate than purchasing a policy. It is important for those considering retirement. [83] Those who live out their lives in a nursing home may consume all of their savings and assets, including their home. After this, the state-run health programs such as Medicaid step in and pay the bills. Unfortunately, you have to be broke before this occurs.

In **summary** here is a final checklist to focus on the issues and ideas in this chapter.

It is likely I will owe income tax on my:	Yes	No
• **Personal savings**		
• **Pension**		
• **Social Security**		

---

[83] http://www.aarp.org/health/health-insurance/info-06-2012/understanding-long-term-care-insurance.html

	Yes	No
I have a budget for retirement		
My budget includes allocation for:		
• Income Tax		
• Property Tax		
• Health Insurance		
• Long-term care insurance		
• Medicine		
• Personal allowances		
I am or will be enrolled in:		
• Medicare Part A		
• Medicare Part B		
• Medicare Part C (Medicare Advantage Plan)		
• Medicare D (drug plan)		
• Gap insurance		
I have consolidated my assets		
I have a sheet which lists assets and liabilities		
I have or will have a: • Will • Living Trust		

Chapter Four

Building Your Lifestyle: What are you going to do with your time?

You made it. You did it. You planned for it. And you can afford it. Now, what are you going to do with your time?   It does not take long for the successful retiree to wonder how they ever had time for a job.

Retirement can be full of so many things. You will not have to consider a post-career schedule of morning news and cooking shows on TV, followed by afternoon talk shows and evening sit-coms and old movies. Retirement is something that is active so do not allow it to be passive. Retirement is something you do, not something imposed on you. You are in control of your life for as long as you live.   You can grab it and fulfill dreams and passions. You can do things not done and become who you always meant to be. When a retiree realizes the new choices, he or she is overwhelmed.

J. thought that retirement would bring a wonderful freedom from schedules and commitments. No longer would vacation time have to be planned to fit around D.'s work.   They could just pick up and go whenever they wanted. Not so! After a busy professional life, D. was apprehensive that he would not have enough to occupy him during retirement. Their new community offered an abundance of activities. He was like a kid in the candy store and he wanted to sample a bit of everything. Instead of being as free as a bird, J. felt she was a caged bird, held in check by a new set of responsibilities and schedules.

This is the side of retirement that defies analysis.   We have discussed social, psychological and financial readiness for retirement. Preparing for retirement should never be an obsession, but it should be in one's thinking early in a career.   Once it occurs, you can be suddenly struck with a gripping realization: "I am mortal." "What can I yet do to become a better person?" It is possible you are everything you wanted to be and perhaps even more. Watching television and reading books may be all you want to do. But if there are personality warts and mental quirks that have yet to be resolved, retirement is a good time to work on them. If there are dreams, fantasies or goals that are unfulfilled, now is the time to explore them and either attain those goals or admit that you will not or no longer care to. Retirement is time to sleep, if you wish, watch television, if you wish, but also time to take yoga classes, begin golf and tennis lessons, learn square dancing, practice woodworking and candlestick making, attend law school or seminary or volunteer for Habitat for Humanity or Salvation Army.

> *K. wanted to get in better shape when he retired. Since he was diabetic, he knew proper diet and physical exercise would prevent his disease from progressing. His partner, G., however wanted to take up line dancing. Six months into their retirement, K. was still going to the gym twice a week while G. had moved on to acrylic painting and Native American flute playing.*

Building a Healthy Lifestyle Through Good Nutrition Retirement is time to live a healthy life and become physically active and fit. This means good nutrition. There are innumerable articles in magazines about eating "healthy". The U.S. Department of Agriculture has guidelines on proper diet [84] Good nutrition is common sense. Taken in moderation, there is probably no food that is inherently bad for you. A simple guideline is "eat color". Bright, colored foods are healthier for you, greens, reds, yellows and oranges, than are whites, beiges and grays. Numerous daily servings of vegetables and fruits are excellent since they have vitamins and minerals. They provide necessary fiber to keep your digestive tract regular. Servings of bread, cereal, rice and pasta are the best sources of carbohydrates, the substance that provides energy for your body. Milk, cheese and yogurt group are important, too, you do not need as much of these in a day as you do grains, vegetables and fruit.. You do not need lots of fats, oils and sweets so you should seldom eat them. Attention to food intake and good nutrition is the basis of continued

---

[84] http://www.washingtonpost.com/wp-srv/nation/daily/graphics/diet_042005.html

good health. Good and consistent nutrition translates into reduced illness and trips to the doctor. It might even reduce your medical expenses.

Building a Healthy Lifestyle Through Weight Control. You are what you eat. If you eat too much and exercise too little, you will be overweight. Being overweight limits mobility and stresses joints and muscles. The condition can result in major health problems and risks as you age, including high blood pressure, type 2 diabetes, gallbladder and liver disease, osteoarthritis, stroke, heart disease, some types of cancer and sleep apnea.

If you are overweight when you retire, take the weight off gradually through a program of good nutrition and exercise. Do not jump from one fad diet to the next. How tragic it would be to have done all your financial homework for retirement and have it blighted by medical problems due to being overweight.

How do you know if you are overweight? There used to be charts that showed a range of weight for one's height and body type (small, medium or large frame). Recently, body mass index (BMI)[85] has replaced the charts.

BMI is calculated in this manner: [86]
1. Take your body weight in pounds and multiply it by 703
2. Divide that by the square of your height in inches

> *S. is 5'2' and weighs 100 pounds. Her BMI is determined as: (100 x 703) divided by (62 x 62) = 70300 divided by 3844 = 18.28 (BMI). Her sister is also 5'2' but weighs 150 pounds. Her BMI is determined as: (150 x 703) divided by (62 x 62) = 10545 divided by 3844 = 27.4. S. is slightly below weight while her sister is marginally overweight.*

---

[85] https://en.wikipedia.org/wiki/Body_mass_index
[86] http://www.whathealth.com/bmi/formula.html

A BMI between 19.1-25.8 is healthy, so the first example represents a person slightly underweight . A BMI between 25.8-32.3 is overweight, as seen in the second example. A BMI of 32.3 or higher is obese. This scale has been used by the World Health Organization to assess many areas of the world for pandemic malnutrition as well as obesity, using different norms for each area. For Americans the norms are: [87]

Condition	BMI in women	BMI in men
Below the weight	< 19.1	< 20.7
Normal weight	19.1 - 25.8	20.7 - 26.4
Marginally overweight	25.8 - 27.3	26.4 - 27.8
Overweight	27.3 - 32.3	27.8 - 31.1
Obese	> 32.3	> 31.1

In retirement, weight loss and control can be more systematic than when you worked and ate lunch out every day. You may find that you eat a later breakfast and an earlier dinner, totally eliminating lunch. This is a good schedule in retirement. If you are hungry between meals, graze on fruits, nuts and vegetables. We are healthier with smaller meals more frequently. Two major meals a day with snacks between is a good way to control and even lose weight.

Building a Healthy Lifestyle Through Physical Fitness Exercise is an important aspect of retirement. If you sit, you atrophy. Do not begin an exercise program before you consult your doctor and be certain to include stretching as your first and last ritual each time. A simple and brisk walk for 45-60 minutes 3-4 times a week is relaxing and helpful for overall muscle flexibility. It can also reward you aesthetically with a feeling of well

---

[87] http://www.nhlbi.nih.gov/health/educational/lose_wt/BMI/bmicalc.htm

being from being in shape. Bicycling is good exercise for seniors. You do not need to go fast since the number of revolutions you turn the sprocket is the test of what you are accomplishing. Although jogging is a good exercise if you have been doing it, it is hard on your knees and legs. It is better to visit a fitness center and use a treadmill, an elliptical trainer or a cross-country ski machine. Pickleball [88] is a racket sport that provides a workout for former tennis and racket ball players whose knees and hips no longer can endure a rigorous sport. There are many ways to stay fit. It is good to do lots of things, to cross train. You will never become bored with one activity. The key is consistency.

Weight training is good to maintain body strength and muscle tone. One needs neither a large number of routines nor heavy weights. A simple set of dumb bells can provide what you need to keep muscles flexible and firm. As you work with weights, body fat is replaced with muscle. Your weight will not necessarily decrease. But you will be stronger and the muscles will support your bone structure.

Fitness centers encourage retirees to join. Group classes provide activities such as aerobics, core training, Pilates [89] and T'ai Chi. [90] The social atmosphere of a health club is a great motivator to begin and stick with a fitness program.

> *K. had experienced low-back pain for twenty years and had used a variety of prescription medications, including Cox-2 inhibitors, to mitigate the pain. He eventually enrolled in a first-level Pilates class with the hope of strengthening his core. Although it took several sessions to unlock his tight muscles, he began to see progress in his posture and range of motion. Over time, the pain and muscle spasms diminished.*

---

[88] http://www.usapa.org/what-is-pickleball/

[89] http://www.mayoclinic.org/healthy-lifestyle/fitness/in-depth/pilates-for-beginners/art-20047673

[90] http://www.taichiforseniorsvideo.com/?gclid=CK-Wu5ebr8kCFYqIfgodqRgOCw

Alcohol. For many, it is tempting in retirement to anticipate the cocktail hour each day. Drinking among older Americans [91] has always been a problem. When working, you probably did not indulge in the evening cocktail each day. In retirement, it is tempting. The longer the person has been retired, the greater the temptation to begin the cocktail hour earlier and earlier.

There is a rule to follow with drinking in retirement. Do it only before dinner and limit your intake to one drink, defined as 5 oz. of wine, 12 oz. of beer or 1.5 oz. of distilled spirits, not all you can pour into one glass. This is moderate use of alcohol for older people. [92] It is a relaxing denouement to a day of accomplishing satisfying goals before you have dinner.

The same rule applies to parties. One drink, eat and then stop. It controls your weight, your personality and prevents addiction. The interaction of alcohol with medications can be devastating. Alcohol abuse contributes to medical conditions such as liver disease, ulcers, high blood pressure and depression. And there is always the danger of falling and fracturing vital body structures while under the influence.

Sleep. You need good sleep. And you need as much as you did when you were working, 7 to 8 hours per night. [93] It is harder to achieve when you are older because you sleep lighter and may wake up several times per night. If you cannot sleep the required amount during the night, nap during the day. Insomnia comes from stress, anxiety, caffeine, or alcohol. Prescription drugs may cause it. Thinking about insomnia ("I'm not going to fall asleep.") even causes insomnia.

If pain or impairment is causing chronic insomnia, the doctor can help. If occasional insomnia is the issue, there are easy solutions. Stick to a consistent time to go to bed and

---

[91] https://www.nia.nih.gov/health/publication/alcohol-use-older-people
[92] http://www.mayoclinic.org/healthy-lifestyle/nutrition-and-healthy-eating/in-depth/alcohol/art-20044551
[93] http://www.comfortkeepers.com/home/info-center/senior-health-wellbeing/seniors-and-sleep-how-much-do-they-need

a time to rise. Never sleep in. Avoid staying up later than usual. Make certain your bedroom is cool and quiet. Do not watch television or use the computer right before you go to bed; rather, unwind somehow, such as reading, listening to music, or taking a warm bath. Relax and do not worry about sleeping. Deprogram yourself an hour before bedtime and insomnia may no longer be a problem. Retirees who are physically fit have better sleep patterns. But a heavy workout before going to bed is not advisable either. It is better to take a stroll through your neighborhood after dinner and then relax. And totally avoid sleeping pills, whether over-the-counter or prescribed. They lead to dependency.

Retirement may require you to change your sleep times. It is best to sleep primarily at night, but you may want both to retire and rise earlier.

Building an Active Lifestyle. You may have always wanted to be the boss or the CEO. Congratulations. In retirement, you are your own CEO. You answer to yourself. The success of retirement is not doing less, but doing as much or more. It is easy to take an hour to do a five-minute job. Before you retired, you might have tried doing the five-minute job in one. Now you can take the full five minutes.

Good retirement is active, not passive. You create things for yourself to do rather than reacting to what others are telling you to do. It means planning your day so that things are accomplished that you wish. It also means you do them in the time you want. You can be active by saying: "Today I'll wash the car, then I'll read the newspaper. After that, I'll go to the fitness center for an hour. In the afternoon, I'll tackle that spot on the front cement and adjust the touchy window in the bedroom. Then I'll do some surfing on the Internet to find out more about the major Pacific campaigns in World War II that my uncle served in. After dinner, I want to watch part of the DVD of "Lord of the Rings" and read a little more before I go to bed." If you do not do all of this, tomorrow you try again. No one is keeping score.

Unlike active retirement, passive retirement is letting others control what you do. It might be spending endless hours on the phone with friends discussing much of nothing. It might be joining your friends for golf to fill out a foursome that had lost a member at the last minute. It might be shopping trips to check out something that could be better handled online. And it includes watching television and channel surfing because you cannot think of anything else to do.

Active retirement requires a plan, a rough blueprint of what you hope to achieve in a day. It also means making plans for courses you want to take, objectives you want to achieve and places you want to travel in the next months or years. Staying alive and breathing in and out is not a goal that needs to be cited. Passive retirement is letting life wash over you without setting your own agenda. Retirement does not mean you stop doing and learning things. It means you plan what you want to do with your partner, if you have one, and make it happen. That is an active lifestyle.

D. and J. approached retirement with different expectations and had to adjust to these differences. Had they remained in their hand-crafted dream home in Georgia, he expected to spend his retirement years developing the property into a horticultural showplace, puttering away in his workshop to build gazebos, garden swings and benches to tuck away in hidden enclaves among the trees and flowers. With the remaining time, he envisioned joining choirs and singing groups to indulge a talent too long suppressed. Rejoining community theater groups was part of his dream, or maybe taking an active role in facilitating men's groups or spiritual workshops. Time would be devoted to reading, or just watching the spring-fed stream trickle over Picnic Rock a few feet from his back door.

J.'s vision seemed to require moving, which they ultimately agreed to do, from the home that they had spent 25 years carving out of the wilderness. No more hard physical labor for her! They should move to a ready-made community where the yard work and maintenance requirements were minimal: an insular, self-contained community where activities were available, but where one felt safe and free to sit in splendid isolation, reading, painting and contemplating. The few domestic chores would be equally divided between them.

Building a Self-Fulfilling Lifestyle. What passions do you have? What do you want to know? What skills do you want to develop? Where do you want to be in five years? What kind of person do you want to become? Retirement is the time when you answer these questions and act on their fulfillment. A self-inventory is a good starting place. Here is a guide:

What do I do now that I want to keep doing?	
How can I become better at these things?	
What new things do I want to master?	

How will I begin?	
1. **Self-instruction**	
2. **Internet Research**	
3. **Class at a Community College**	
What wild and crazy thing do I want to do in retirement?	
What are my goals for next week?	
1.	
2. .	
3.	
What are my goals for the next year?	
1.	
2.	
3.	
What are my goals for the next five years?	
1.	
2.	
3.	

What kind of person am I? (What would people say about me?)	
What kind of person would I like to become? (Or what would I like written on my tombstone?)	
How will I accomplish this?	

This self-inventory is useful for anyone, even those just beginning or sustaining in the workforce. For retirees, it is critical. You are responsible for success and happiness in retirement. Although others controlled your time and energies when you were employed, now you are master of your time and energies. You are the CEO of a company called MSR, Inc. (My Successful Retirement). Plan it well. Revise that plan as you live and develop. And keep setting five-year goals for as long as you live.

> *When P. was asked what she did in retirement, she responded: " I belong to a putting group, the Verde Sputters, meet with a good friend from the college every month for lunch and a movie, teach clogging as a volunteer to a group of nine women, bicycle, motorcycle, travel, utilize our timeshares, read, take computer classes, visit with my two sons in North Carolina and Reno, and my two stepsons in Maine. I also manage to enjoy my grandchildren as much as possible."*

Building an Enriched Lifestyle. You retired because you had enough funds to do so and were ready. What are you going to do to enrich that lifestyle so that one day does not become much like the next? There are so many things in which to be involved without a job that this section could be limitless. Here are a few possibilities.

Internet Exploration. The Internet has placed the world's libraries at your fingertips. With high-speed access, you can surf to your heart's content and never exhaust the possibilities to learn and read. Although it is fun to surf, a good strategy for systematically improving your knowledge is to list subjects you want to pursue. Each day or each time your have an extended Internet session, explore all the possibilities of that one area you selected. Keep a sheet, hardcopy or virtual file that you add to as you think of things you want to know:

1. What are the various classes of naval ships? How and where are they constructed? How long does it take? How are they commissioned and named? How long do they remain in the fleet? What happens when they are decommissioned?

2. When was the first jet plane invented? By whom? Where? When did jets first appear in the military? When were they first used in commercial flights? How does a jet engine develop thrust?

3. Who were the monarchs of Russia? How and when did Russia first become a country? What were its boundaries? Who were its people? Who were the greatest monarchs? How were they related to other European dynasties? How did the Russian monarchy end? Are there survivors?

4. How old is the earth? What are the geologic periods that can be identified throughout the history of the earth? What plants or animals were associated with each? Where is evidence of this geological evolution? Is the earth still changing? What evidence is there of these changes?

5. What are the greatest inventions of humankind? When did they occur? What differences did they make to the common people?

If you are a curious person who is always trying to figure out his or her environment, there is no end. Where are there good sources of topics to pursue? You probably have many in your head right now. Jot them down. Reading newspapers and magazines will stimulate your curiosity. Movies and live theatre do the same. Discovery and history channels on TV are sources to stimulate your curiosity.

Let us assume you have seen a production of *Macbeth* on stage. This might stimulate you to pursue Shakespeare on the Internet to see what other tragedies he wrote and when. Questions you might want answers for include: Were the tragedies based on historical events or personages? How have these been adapted for modern settings? Why do they have relevance for today's viewers? How do they compare to Shakespeare's histories? His comedies? Did he really write them?

How are you going to use this knowledge? You probably are not going to deliver it to others, that is, unless you want to be the insufferable bore at every dinner party. It is merely a scheme to keep your mind active as well as satisfying natural curiosity. In retirement, you can pursue these fields. To some people, it may be trivia. To you, it is enrichment and understanding.

This worksheet might be useful to assess your areas of interest:

Area of Curiosity	Questions I Want To Answer
I.	1.
	2.
	3.
	4.
	5.
	6.

II.	1.
	2.
	3.
	4.
	5.
	6.
III.	1.
	2.
	3.
	4.
	5.
	6.
IV.	1.
	2.
	3.
	4.
	5.
	6.
V.	1.
	2.
	3.
	4.
	5.
	6.

Volunteering. To this mission of enrichment can be added activities that make you grow as a person. Volunteering is an excellent way to develop skills and knowledge. Some volunteering requires "grunt" work that no one else will do: sorting old clothes, answering a phone, or greeting people at a store. But other types require training and skill.

A. volunteers at church, hikes, plays cards with a bridge group, and like all retirees, travels more extensively. In her words: "When I retired, I started dancing, which was my way of fulfilling a dream I had when I was a kid of becoming a Rockette! While all of this is good, what I think is the most satisfying is that I started tutoring math right away, and continue to do so at the local junior/senior high school. This gives me a feeling of accomplishment, which everyone needs."

Becoming a docent at a museum, gallery or zoo requires you to learn about the facility and what it contains as well as how to convey the knowledge. Federal and state park systems use volunteers as guides and interpreters. Medical facilities need volunteers to help patients with non-medical tasks. Elementary schools need volunteers to hear kids read and to assist classroom teachers. Volunteering can be a rewarding, growing experience. One needs a spirit of altruism. In addition, you will get something from the experience, including new knowledge and skills in dealing with people, product or service. There are even opportunities to volunteer in other countries.

If in doubt where to begin, simply type "Volunteer Opportunities" on your Internet search engine. You will find a wealth of information for locating volunteer opportunities.[94] According to VolunteerMatch, the Internet is second only to word-of-mouth for locating a volunteer position. Over 4 million individuals used this means in 2008.[95]

F. always surveyed the "Volunteers Needed" column in his Sunday paper to see what was available. Twice he called and went to an agency, which needed volunteers and found himself stuffing envelopes and licking stamps, which, he deemed, was a bit inappropriate for a former

---

[94]
https://en.wikipedia.org/wiki/VolunteerMatch
[95]*Ibid.*

corporation lawyer. "Why volunteer to do jobs the regular workers don't want to do?" Then he discovered the conference to which his church belonged supported a mission in Mexico, which needed volunteers. These involved collecting household items, including clothing, repairing them and then going to Mexico on a bus for a weekend to deliver these goods to needy families. It was a volunteer job that required thinking and skill. In addition, he got to use the Spanish he was learning at the local community college.

Travel. Travel is a good way to grow in retirement. Most retirees think of travel as the 21-day cruise to Micronesia, but there are travel possibilities in your own area. Have you visited all the museums and galleries in the town where you live? Chances are, tourists who come to your city visit these. Become a tourist in your own town and visit museums, botanical gardens, art galleries, military bases and auto exhibitions. The trip to Micronesia is a nice dream but there are smaller trips in your own location to explore. How many interesting things are available to visit within an hour's drive from your home? Two hours' drive? Have you seen them all? Retirement is the time to do it.

If you are able to travel wider and further, consider what you can see by train or bus. Airplanes are the glamour way to travel, but train or bus will get you there as well if not as quickly. Most depots are located in city centers where you can rent a car or walk to nearby hotels. Avoid big cities and have a small town experience. Some of the best travel memories will come from a small town fiesta or 4th of July parade. You can even arrange a Bed and Breakfast in many areas. There is the possibility of house sitting for someone in a new area, which would greatly reduce costs, or even doing a house-exchange.   Trips do not have to be long. They do not have to be to exotic places. A few days' travel can put you into a new environment where you can learn how people live in a different town.

Here are some interesting things to find out about any town you might visit:

- What is the population?
- What are the main industries?
- Have there ever been other industries?
- How do people make a living in this town?
- Are there colleges in the town?
- What is the average price of a home?
- Why is the town famous?
- What stories and legends are there about the town?
- Are there museums and galleries?
- When was the town founded? By whom?
- What is the racial mix?
- How is the town governed?
- Is this town growing, sustaining or dying? Why?

You can research this on the Internet either before or after your visit. It is always interesting to ask people you meet during your visit to see what they know about the town.

Educational Courses. Formal education is an enriching experience for many retirees. Short of earning a college degree, there are numerous courses available in local universities and community colleges. These might be short-term language courses to provide basic fluency in Spanish, before you visit Mexico, or French, before you visit Quebec. You might want to take a short course in computer software, such as Quicken or Quick Books (to help manage your budget), Microsoft Word (to help you write better), or Photoshop (to help process and enhance digital photos.) Community colleges are less expensive than universities and the enrollment process is simpler.

Many colleges offer Elderhostel classes that include day trips, short-term single-focus classes, and travel experiences. Elderhostel is usually inexpensive for travel and tuition. Since it is an international program, which includes 90 countries, one could go from one place to another, using Elderhostel. Participants often stay on a college campus in a dormitory room and eat meals in the cafeteria. Founded in 1975, Elderhostel (Road Scholar) offers programs for adults, 55 and over, both in the U.S. and abroad. [96] It is a way to link with other retirees who share interests and values in programs that are edifying and fun.

Cultural Activities. Involvement with the arts is a worthy use of time in retirement. Centuries ago, Goethe stated that the arts provide entertainment, edification and exaltation. That is no less true today than it was when he made this statement. We are entertained in a noble sense by involvement with the arts. We are edified because we learn something about the creative process, which helps us understand ourselves. And there is an element of exaltation with every great work of art, a form of magic that moves us through gesture, sound, color and form in profound ways we do not always understand.

What does involvement with the arts imply? You can be a spectator or you can be a participant. You can attend opera, theatre, cinema, ballet and art exhibits. If ticket prices are too high, your local college or university has high quality events at discount prices. You can also do it yourself, that is, take a class that teaches you to paint, to tap dance, to play the recorder or to edit a video. If you are a singer, there are church and community choirs, as well as roles in musicals and operas. If you are an actor, community theatre always needs talent, if not to act, to paint sets and work lights. You might even understudy a lead and have your chance on opening night! If you play a band or orchestra instrument, civic groups would welcome you. Will you have to practice? Yes, but now you have time.

Sports. Much as in the arts, you can be a spectator or a participant. There are many professional and semi-professional sporting activities in many communities. Local high schools have sporting events to attend. And although you may not be able to play touch football anymore, golf, tennis and pickleball are good senior activities. In addition, the

---

[96] http://www.roadscholar.org/about/history.asp

Senior Olympics [97] is a way to be involved in competition, regardless of age. Sponsored by the National Senior Games Association, the goal helps participants live a healthy lifestyle. Over a quarter million seniors participate annually in games, which include archery, badminton, basketball, bowling, cycling, golf, horseshoes, racewalk, racquetball, road race, shuffleboard, softball, swimming, table tennis, tennis, track and field, triathlon and volleyball.

Personality Type. An important consideration that affects how and what you will do in retirement to enrich your life is personality type. If you have never participated in a personality test, the Myers Briggs Type Indicator [98] is an excellent place to begin. You will determine whether you are an introvert or an extrovert. This has nothing to do with whether you are social or not, but rather in which environment you recharge your batteries. Introverts enjoy doing things by themselves while extroverts get energy from others. There is no inherent value in either personality type but it does help one understand what you might enjoy doing and how. Bicycling by oneself is typical of an introvert's approach to sports whereas an extrovert enjoys group classes and golf foursomes.

Another personality test is True Colors [99] which provides a slightly different view of one's self. Neither test is to be taken as a self-fulfilling prophecy, but helps us understand ourselves. We should broaden our tastes, preferences and activities, particularly in senior years. Not only will we understand ourselves, we will understand those who live and play around us.

Summary. There are too many things to do in retirement to do them all. If you do a personal inventory, you will find that your days will be full. We have not said anything about the joy that will come from reading. A morning newspaper that can be read thoroughly instead of merely skimmed over a cup of coffee is an adventure most people

---

[97] http://www.nsga.com
[98] http://www.myersbriggs.org/my-mbti-personality-type/mbti-basics/
[99] https://truecolorsintl.com/about-us/what-is-true-colors/

who have spent 30 or more years in the workforce have not experienced. Similarly, pursuing a favorite novelist and reading all of his and her works can be done. Thoroughly reading magazines that used to accumulate because you did not have time to touch them will be part of your retirement if you enjoy that.

We can add involvement with civic and church groups. There is meaning in group purpose and in sharing your faith, social skills and energies with a Senior Sunday School class, the Rotarians or B.P.O.E. (Elks) as part of your retirement. To avoid recreating workplace commitments, though, it is well not to oversubscribe to any one activity or group. If you do, you will be experiencing the same pressures and commitments you experienced while employed. If that is what you want, why retire? Do not substitute one set of pressures for others for which you are not paid. Easily come and go in retirement and do not tie yourself down. Re-evaluate your retirement commitments frequently to be certain you have not replaced a job for which you were paid for jobs in which you are not paid. A happy balance keeps you feeling purposeful without being chained down.

A. offered this to women retirees: "Here is a piece of advice for women when their husband also retires. "Don't take your husband grocery shopping with you. He will want to push the cart (I think it's a control thing!) and what woman can think in the grocery store without hanging on to the cart? But if he wants to go on his own, that's great'."

Here is a summary to help you plan and focus what you're going to do with your new freedom in retirement.

Activity or Interest	Level of Interest 1 (Very Low) 2 (Low) 3 (Medium) 4 (High) 5 (Very High)	Willingness to Do 1 (Very Low) 2 (Low) 3 (Medium) 4 (High) 5 (Very High)
Healthy Lifestyle	1 2 3 4 5	1 2 3 4 5

Good Nutrition	1	2	3	4	5	1	2	3	4	5
Weight Control	1	2	3	4	5	1	2	3	4	5
Physical Fitness	1	2	3	4	5	1	2	3	4	5
Alcohol Control	1	2	3	4	5	1	2	3	4	5
Sleep	1	2	3	4	5	1	2	3	4	5
Active Lifestyle	1	2	3	4	5	1	2	3	4	5
Self-Fulfilling Lifestyle	1	2	3	4	5	1	2	3	4	5
Enriched Lifestyle	1	2	3	4	5	1	2	3	4	5
Internet Exploration	1	2	3	4	5	1	2	3	4	5
Volunteering	1	2	3	4	5	1	2	3	4	5
Travel	1	2	3	4	5	1	2	3	4	5
Educational Courses	1	2	3	4	5	1	2	3	4	5
Cultural Activities	1	2	3	4	5	1	2	3	4	5
• **Art**	1	2	3	4	5	1	2	3	4	5
• **Theatre**	1	2	3	4	5	1	2	3	4	5
• **Music**	1	2	3	4	5	1	2	3	4	5
• **Cinema**	1	2	3	4	5	1	2	3	4	5
• **Dance**	1	2	3	4	5	1	2	3	4	5
Sports	1	2	3	4	5	1	2	3	4	5

Chapter Five

Can you be a part-time worker?

R. had certainly put in her time for public education. She taught 5 years before her first child was born, was off for 8 years until all the children were in Kindergarten in her own district, and then returned to the classroom for another 24 years before retiring. She promised the district she would substitute whenever they called. They called and called, consistently early on Monday mornings. She thought a few days of substituting here and there would be fun, but she found herself back into the schools most days of the week, attending staff meetings and pulling bus duty. Is this what she really wanted in retirement?

Former Position. The party celebrating their retirement is over, the weekend is gone. They take the next week for vacation. And the following Monday, they are back in the office doing what they did before they announced they were retiring. There is one difference. They receive 30% of their former salary for working a day and a half. Actually, they are drawn into the workplace 3 or 4 days a week. Nonetheless, many retirees continue as part-timers at their former employment because they find it hard to let go of the status, respect, empowerment and money they enjoyed.

Why do retirees return to their former employment? Your boss says you are needed for transition? You cannot give it up? You need the money? You cannot let go? Your co-workers miss and need you? Your spouse cannot stand having you at home? You actually may have more income from your pension, Social Security and the part-time company check. There is a shift in your funding source, but you are still working.

How many pre-retirees plan to work after retirement? And why do retirees continue to work? According to a survey, 50% of retirees continue to work part-time. [100] The survey states that staying active and being useful is a strong motivation. As the Boomers continue to retire, there may be more jobs available than workers to fill them. The generation following Boomers is smaller, leaving positions unfilled. There are 78 million Boomers but only 46 million Gen X'ers. [101] Because of the shift in demographics, as well as hiring practices of many companies, there are more jobs than workers, providing opportunities for part-time work.

Why retire and come back to the same job? Officially retiring gives you balance between work and personal life. You have more control on what you will do and even when you will do it. This can be important to meet personal needs in your life. Thirty percent of all retirees 65 or older are caregivers for a spouse, parent or even a grandchild. [102]

Is it ever prudent to continue working part-time for your former employer? Certainly, if you have critical skills that are part of the training for your replacement. But this is a short-term assignment. It lasts 2-3 months and you move out and on. Part-time work for your former employer can be something other than doing what you did before you retired. If you need income, can your job be done by telecommuting? Can you work from home? Can you be involved in special projects? Can you be a temporary or relief worker in another department?

Many pre-retirees want to learn something new, so a different assignment with the old employer might be the answer. It would mitigate the constant: "But I thought you retired" banter that occurs when you return after the retirement party. Other workers get skeptical about your double dipping. But since only one-third of all pre-retirees look forward to a life of retirement without work, the other two-thirds believe work is important and will continue working into their seventies.

---

[100] http://www.thefiscaltimes.com/2015/11/02/Here-s-Why-So-Many-Retirees-Are-Still-Working
[101] http://www.napavalley.edu/people/jhall/Documents/Generational%20Chart.pdf
[102] https://www.caregiver.org/selected-long-term-care-statistics

Tax Consequences. If you are drawing Social Security, part-time work may affect your benefits. There are limits on what you can earn while on Social Security without losing some benefits. If you retire before your full retirement age (65, if born in 1937 or earlier, but gradually increasing, as described in Chapter 2, to age 67 if born 1960 or later), you may earn $15,720 in 2015 without losing benefits. If you earn more from a part-time job, you forfeit $1 in benefits for every $2 you earn over the limit. [103] If you were on benefits in 2015 and earned $18,000, your benefit would be reduced $1140 or $95 per month.

W. was born in January 1950 and retired January 2015 at 65. His official retirement age is 66, which will be January 2016. If he begins to draw Social Security benefits when he retires and continues to work part-time, he may earn $15,720 without penalty. However, since he is taking benefits 1 year before his full retirement age when his projected benefit would be $1600 a month, his benefit will be $1492.80, 93.3% of what it would be at age 66.

There is good news, however. In the year you reach full retirement age, you can earn $41,880 (2015) in the months before your reach that age. If you earn over that amount, the penalty is $1 for every $3 you earn. Thus, if in the months of the year before you reach your full retirement age you earn $50,000 (2015), you would lose $2707 in benefits or $226 per month. The penalty is not forever. It affects benefits for the next year. After full retirement age, you may earn without limit or penalty. Nonetheless, there is a high price for drawing Social Security and working part-time before you reach full retirement age. [104]

Since W.'s pension provides $40,500 a year, 85% of his Social Security benefits will be taxed. If he accepts his former employer's contract to

---

[103] https://faq.ssa.gov/link/portal/34011/34019/Article/3739/What-happens-if-I-work-and-get-Social-Security-retirement-benefits
[104] *Ibid.*

complete two projects in 2015 for a fee of $22,000, he will lose $3140 in benefits for that year, $262 per month, reducing his Social Security benefit to $1231.14. Solution: W. should not retire or, if he does, either reject the company's contract or delay Social Security benefits until later, possibly January 2016.

What are options for part-time work? Flextime is an option for many employees through job-share. You share a job with someone, each working 20 hours per week. You fill in for someone on maternity, sick or military leave. If you have the background, you substitute for a school district. You might be a relief worker for those in a company taking scheduled vacations. Flextime and temporary help are a reality of corporate life in America. Large corporations can quickly adjust to changing market conditions with a smaller regular workforce. They supplement it with temp-workers when demand for their service or product rises. The downside for the worker, of course, is there are usually fewer benefits, such as health care. However, as a retiree, you should have that covered with Medicare and gap insurance once you reach full retirement age.

Self-Employment. There is always the option of beginning your own business. For most retirees, this can be more of a pain that a blessing. What skills do you have that can be turned into a productive business? Handyman? Seamstress? Event organizer? House cleaner? Musician? Accountant? Tax preparer? Real estate agent? Interior decorator? Computer trainer and serviceperson? House painter? House sitter and security guard? Web designer? Graphic artist?

It takes time to fill a market niche. One has to analyze a community need and see if that need is being satisfied. If there is a niche, it might be yours for the taking, after you design a business plan and plan your marketing. Even then, your start-up costs might outweigh your eventual earnings. It could be fun and you might meet lots of people, but the risks are high as well. There is the issue of bonding when you do work for other people as well as liability insurance. There is always the fear of lawsuits should you not perform to the standard your clients demand. With your own business, however, your tax position is favorable since many expenses can be deducted on Schedule C, thus lowering income and self-employment taxes. (You would have to pay into Social Security at 15.3%.)

> *One of T.'s dreams, once R. retired, was to open a catering business out of her home. She had catered many neighborhood parties and friends kept referring her to others because of her skill in cuisine and presentation. She also thought a few hundred dollars a month would provide some of the "added" things they might need in retirement. In addition, it was fun to go to beautiful homes and present an exciting meal for her clients and their guests. She developed a business plan, which included marketing on the Internet as well as flyers in the local newspaper. In the first year, she grossed $15,450 in revenue from some 25 parties. Most of her expenses could be itemized on Schedule C of their income tax return and her net profit from these endeavors, that occupied 50-60 days in the year, was $2350. She was doing what she loved to do and did well. In addition, she met lots of interesting, appreciative people.*

Other Options. As a part-timer, you might wish to pursue a new job, one that provides a salary from an employer but does not require you to learn many new skills or to establish a second career. The service industry is the place for you. You can work in a fast-food restaurant by learning to punch up an electronic cash register. Retail stores need greeters and clerks, particularly during the holidays. There are websites that list the top categories for finding part time positions. [105] Among these are web designer, nursing, healthcare, computer programming and accounting. Each requires a level of skill, training and professionalism.

---

[105] http://www.sologig.com

Freelance and short-term contract work is possible too, depending on your background or willingness to invest in further training. The same website lists paralegal, proofreader, illustrator, photographer and web designer as opportunities. [106]

Retirees with backgrounds in business management, software design and networks, the environment and many types of engineering are ready candidates as consultants to industry and government on a part-time basis. If this is your background, it may keep you alive and current in your field without the 40+ hours required of fulltime employment.

Between 50-65% of the readers will seek and find part-time work. It is well to remember why you retired. You were ready and people around you were retiring. You had the financial means to do it. You already had a career, so be careful about a second career, even if it is part-time. The focus of retirement is seldom to begin another career path; rather, it is to keep active and bring in a bit of coin. Enjoying a second cup of coffee on many mornings and the opportunity to read the entire editorial page in the newspaper were reasons you retired. The grueling commute and inane unit meetings are reasons to remain principally retired.

In **summary**, here is a checklist to assist you in planning part-time work

I don't need/want to work part-time.	(Stop here.)	
I need/want to work part-time.	Yes	No
I need/want to work.	_____ hours per week or _____ weeks per year	
I want a job, not a second career.	Yes	No
I want to begin my own business	Yes	No

---

[106] *Ibid.*

I can develop a business plan that turns a profit.	Yes	No
I have skills that will translate into a part-time job.	Yes	No
Among these skills are:	1. 2. 3. 4. 5.	
These skills would be perfect in this type of job:	1. 2. 3. 4. 5.	
My reasons for retiring were:	1. 2. 3. 4. 5.	
My reasons for working part-time are:	1. 2. 3. 4.	
I can still work and fulfill my retirement goals.	Yes	No

Chapter Six

Can you live with your spouse and family?

"I don't have any time for myself anymore", R. lamented to her sister when B. retired. "I used to be able to sew, read the newspaper, visit on the phone, catch Oprah and then leisurely prepare the evening meal for his return from work. Now I finish the breakfast dishes and it's time for lunch. He will not even make a sandwich for himself. We are both putting on weight. And I do not like this notion of the cocktail hour getting earlier and earlier each night."

Now that you are home, have you noticed someone else is living in the house? That is, if you are married or partnered. Who is this other person? Do you know them? What do you have in common? Have you ever spent this much time together? These are relationship issues that retirees face. Whether there have been two of you in the workforce or only one with a stay-at-home spouse, there are tensions that emerge because you are both bouncing around in the same living space.

Spouses. Let's assume it was a partnership where one person worked outside the home and has just retired and the other has been a stay-at-home spouse. How is life going to change in retirement? The stay-at-home spouse has been the homemaker who raised the kids and prepared the meals. The worker was not there most of the time. After 30+ years of working, he or she is at home. The stay-at-home spouse who has undoubtedly had their own schedule all these years now has a person who intrudes on their space and time. This means demands on the bathroom, kitchen or living room occur at the same time. It might also mean it is lunchtime and the stay-at-home has another meal to prepare, in addition to breakfast, however recent that was, and then dinner.

Solution: Two meals a day: a late breakfast and an early dinner. Or, everyone for themselves, or take turns preparing meals. Eat out more often. Otherwise, the stay-at-home, who does not feel the worker ever understood what they did during the day to contribute to the home, feels like a short-order cook. This situation can develop tension.

When D. retired, he no longer spent most of his waking hours commuting and working five days a week. They moved from twelve acres of heavy woods that required endless maintenance to a home on a lot with low maintenance desert landscaping. J. thought they would share the work that was left: house chores, financial bookwork, and the purchase and preparation of food. D. did like grocery shopping because it provided the opportunity to purchase those food items that J. normally would refrain from buying out of concern for their health.

D. spent his hours and days following his bliss while J. was left at home doing the same chores she had always done. Instead of making sure he was fed and had clean clothes to go to work, she focused her energies to make sure that meals were ready at a certain time. D. could be free to leave the house in time to go to whichever group was meeting that morning, afternoon, or evening. J. was stuck at home.

The stay-at-home spouse might have developed interests such as attending an aerobics class, talking on the phone, watching daytime television or even taking a nap. All of that must be accounted for when someone else is in the house. Solution: Let the stay-at-home continue the schedule while the worker develops his or her own schedule. Togetherness is lovely, but after being apart before retirement, it is okay to have separate interests and schedules. You are not one person, but, rather, two with common interests. But you still have many interests your mate may not share.

As T. put it: "Retirement for us has already been a rich, personal-growth experience; we still work at personal time versus together time. We believe that a long-lasting relationship needs both. Each spouse still needs to develop and nurture individual friendships while as a couple we also develop new friends. You bring new things and surprises to the dinner table that way."

There is a corollary here. The stay-at-home may have developed a list of "honey-do" projects for which he or she was just waiting until the worker retired to get done. The newly minted retiree may just want to mellow out for a few days, weeks or longer. He or she did not think the boss at work was going to be replaced by a 24/7 boss at home, dominating life with tasks, schedules and judgments. Solution: Develop a list of tasks to accomplish, but make the timeline for completion reasonable and undemanding. You have the next 25-30 years to get it done. It is a good to have downtime when you first retire. It allows the creative juices to flow and lets you think through how you are going to make retirement stellar.

It is not much different if both spouses have worked. There may be need for greater downtime to re-enter the world of being a human being. Separate schedules are fine as you sort out your retirement lives.

Children. Children and grandchildren can be an issue in retirement. Many pre-retirees and retirees suddenly find their home shared by a "Boomerang" child, one who has come back after graduating from college. [107] This generation of college graduates, who often take more than four years to complete their degrees, is in less of a hurry to become self-sufficient. They may delay looking for a job until they have had a chance to travel or simply recover from college years. They may work a mindless job until the "right" position becomes available or one in which they are qualified. They marry later, 26.5 for women and 28.7 for men in 2011, [108] and spend their 20s in a variety of living arrangements, including their parents' home. This was once considered a sign of failure, but it is now commonplace. Around 25 million, age 18-31, live with their parents. [109]

---

[107] http://connection.ebscohost.com/c/articles/4642109/echo-Boomerang
[108] http://mic.com/articles/92361/the-median-age-of-marriage-in-every-state-in-the-u-s-in-two-maps#.a2OngincV
[109] http://www.infowars.com/29-percent-of-all-u-s-adults-under-the-age-of-35-are-living-with-their-parents/

The reason? Student debt, lack of employment and the high cost of living. [110] In addition, some children move home because of financial difficulties or divorce.

If your child has a good job, household expenses can be shared, helping you with the retirement budget. Young people move home to maintain the good life style they have enjoyed. Many college graduates have student debt [111] from tuition expenses and this is a way to pay it down. Many want to purchase new cars and electronic equipment that would not be possible if they suddenly had to pay rent and utilities themselves. Many want to save for graduate school or a house while enjoying the comforts of home.

> *C. and S. had been empty nesters for over four years. Suddenly, S. Jr. decided he was going to move back into their home. Rents were too expensive in the city, what with the payments on his student loans, credit card debt, new sports car and flat-screen TV. Although his accounting degree was fresh, his first job had not produced the salary he thought would be forthcoming upon graduation. Needless to say, C. and S. Sr. were less than exhilarated by this turn of events, but many of their friends had already experienced the phenomenon of "Boomerang" kids.*

> *A deal was struck. S. Jr. would pay something for room and board. He would do his own laundry as well as let them know when he was "sleeping" over at a friend's house. Although he could entertain guests, including girl friends, there would be no "sleep overs" in their house. S. Jr. stayed three months and decided he really could afford his own .*

There are guidelines to make this intrusion into your retirement life, however welcome, manageable and equitable. The young adult should contribute to the welfare of the house, paying something for rent, utilities and food. This does not have to be full value,

---

[110] *Ibid.*
[111] http://blogs.wsj.com/economics/2015/05/08/congratulations-class-of-2015-youre-the-most-indebted-ever-for-now/

but should be more than mere token. He or she should participate in the duties of the household, assisting with care giving, if that is an issue, and doing chores or repairs. There should be an agreement how long this arrangement endures, whether a few months or a few years.

The social life of the young adult can be a problem. Although parents would be remiss in insisting on curfews, there is a responsibility to those with whom one lives, even parents. Parents would be perfectly correct in insisting there be notification if the young adult is late or sleeping over with friends. Dating patterns should be articulated. If sleepover dates and raucous parties are not sanctioned, it should be stated. As a parent, the house is yours. You can specify the type of behavior that must occur for the privilege of living there.

Grandchildren. If married children live near you, you may be asked to participate in the upbringing of the grandchildren. This can be babysitting as well as attending school functions and sporting events. This is good for the welfare of your extended family. Your grandchildren will know you. But do not build your life around your grandkids, such as always arranging travel so you do not miss a birthday, holiday or important event. This could consume your entire retirement. You would never get to do what you want to do. Be an important part of their life and see them from time to time. But do not be surrogate parents.

Now that B. was widowed, she longed to be closer to her family. Her three daughters lived in the Midwest, far from the retirement community she and M. had chosen in the Southwest. She lamented she could not see her grandchildren often and they were growing up without her. Although there was ample support in her community for single seniors, including assisted-living arrangement, if and when that became necessary, she sold her home for a loss. She put everything in storage and moved back to the Midwest, to reside in a fourth bedroom in her middle daughter's home until she could find more permanent arrangements. Unfortunately everyone was busy during weekdays with work, school and day care. Since her daughter's family was used to snacking and grazing for supper, B.'s sit down meals were not appreciated. In the evening, the grandchildren did homework or participated in sports and clubs. She did not have as much time with the grandkids as she had assumed. Her son-in-law was becoming a bit hostile to her presence in the home. She felt hemmed in and isolated staying in her small bedroom.

Unfortunately, grandparents raise grandchildren all too frequently. The 2010 United States Census reported 4.9 million children were being raised by grandparents, a figure which doubled from the 2000 census. This may not have been part of someone's retirement plan but all of a sudden, there it is. The most common reasons grandparents take over parenting is because the parent(s) is into drugs (nearly half of the cases), the parents are in prison or the home environment is poor. Child abuse and abandonment are common. Sometimes the parent is too young to raise the child. In rare cases, the parent has died. [112] As a result, 6% of all children in the U.S. are living with a grandparent. [113]

What are guidelines for retirees who face this? There are legal and medical issues beyond the scope of this book. The best advice is to affiliate with a support group since this a growing social problem. Faced with a major role as caregiver, there are useful coping strategies. Do not assign blame and do not hold yourself responsible for your child who did not become a good parent. See things as they really are and work through the issues. Keep your health routine and schedule quiet time away from grandchildren. You need time to recharge your batteries. Follow good nutrition for the children and yourself. Take parenting classes with similarly situated retirees to build a support network as well as to learn new child development techniques. Continue to develop your sense of humor and patience. [114]

---

[112] https://www.womenshealth.gov/aging/caregiving/raising-children-again.html
[113] http://www.retirewow.com/grandparents-raising-grandchildren-increasing-numbers/
[114] http://www.helpguide.org/articles/grandparenting/grandparents-as-parents.htm

Loss of a Spouse. Many retirees lose a spouse in their golden years. This is particularly tragic if retirement had been a dream for two when only one remains. Divorce among retirees 65 or older is low, but rising. In 1990, it was 1.4 people for every 1,000 married women, 2.1 for people for every 1,000 married men. Presently it is 5% of all divorces. [115] For the 65+ in remarriage, the divorce rate is three times higher than a first marriage. [116] If you have minimal years left, why spend them in an unhappy marriage?

It is more likely that death will change everything. What is life expectancy in the United States? The good news is this: The older you are, the greater your life expectancy. In 2000, for men it was 74.1 years and 79.5 for women, an overall decrease in the national death rate. In 2010, it was 76.2 for men and 81.0 for women. [117] This decrease was especially marked in five age groups, four of which were people over 55 (55-64, 65-74, 75-84 and over 85).

Although you will have a long retirement with your partner, it is possible the female may outlive the male. More instructive are causes of death. Heredity is always a factor in disease and death, but some of these can be mitigated by good nutrition and healthy lifestyle.

The number one cause of death after 60 is heart disease. It is often paired with or caused by diabetes, high blood pressure, poor diet, physical inactivity and smoking. This is followed in descending order by cancer, stroke, COPD (chronic obstructive lung disease), pneumonia and diabetes. Frequently, these disorders occur in combination, where cause and effect cannot be attributed. Next are accidents, which come from failing eyesight, balance disorders and slow reflexes. A simple fall in the home can eventually lead to death. Auto accidents are in this category as well. Finally, there is septicemia

---

[115] http://seniorplanet.org/gray-divorce-splitting-up-at-65-plus/
[116] *Ibid.*
[117] http://www.cdc.gov/nchs/data/hus/2011/022.pdf

(pathogenic bacteria in the blood), nephritis (inflammation of the kidney) and Alzheimer's. [118]

What can be done to mitigate against causes of death? Short of being born to a family with healthy genes, each retiree can commit to a healthy lifestyle and an accident-reduced home. This means good eating habits, sleep, positive mental attitude and exercise, as well as visits to the doctor for wellness exams. It means maintaining a reasonable body weight for your age. As we age, keeping weight on is more of a problem than keeping it off! It means getting pneumonia and high-dosage flu shots in season, as well as the shingles vaccination. It means care using a step stool or ladder when doing household chores or repairs or simply hiring them done. It means living on minimal medication and functioning on your own as much as possible, even when there is a little pain and discomfort.

There is not a pill that will make you 25 again. It undoubtedly means utmost care when driving, avoiding heavy traffic, eschewing night driving when possible and using partner advice on the road (4 eyes are better than 2). Eventually, it means no longer driving at all and moving to an assisted-living center. We cannot enjoy long retirements if we do not follow lifestyle advice where healthy choices make a difference, in spite of genetics.

Cohabitation. Surviving retirement and living beyond life expectancy requires a network of friends and organizations. Retirees do not need to become hermits to survive. Should you lose a spouse to divorce or death, life will continue. It is likely you will find another mate. You may remarry or cohabit. Many older couples are choosing the latter. Although the 2000 census reported 266,000 couples over 65 (and 9.7 million in total) who cohabit, these figures probably represent a fraction of the trend. Many couples would not report this on their census questionnaire.

Why is cohabitation common among retirees? It does not mean they do not believe in the formal sanction of marriage. Rather, it means they might lose some Social Security

---

[118] http://seniorhealth.about.com/od/deathanddying/tp/cause_death.htm

benefits, medical insurance or even the pension of their former spouse. This would lower their lifestyle considerably. Some have had bad marriages and ugly divorces, mitigating against tying the knot again. There is worry their children would disapprove of a marriage because it might change the outcome of a will or trust. [119]

> *S. certainly did not condone her daughter living with her fiancé six months before they married. But they did marry and have been together for over ten years. Now she is faced with the same issue. With one divorce behind her plus the death of her second husband, she is shy about marriage. She is reticent to reveal her financial arrangement to her boy friend, C., who thinks he should move into her house so they can share expenses. She knows little about his background and less about his family. She does know he has been married once, possibly twice, and has adult children on the West coast. It would be nice to have a man around the house, but he seems to have more skill in overhauling muscle cars than in fixing plumbing. Her friends advise her to be cautious about this move. What will she really gain?*

A generation of pre-retirees and retirees who watched their children co-habit in college or after are now doing it themselves. There were 575,000 seniors over 65 cohabiting, as reported in the 2010 census. [120] Although there is concern what family and neighbors think, it is common.

Consult a lawyer to check the law of where you live. Some states have rules on palimony. Some couples draft a cohabitation agreement, much like a pre-nuptial agreement, outlining rights and responsibilities, including how expenses are shared. This includes medical incapacity or death, where a durable medical power of attorney is critical. Children from both partners must be involved in these decisions. Otherwise,

---

[119] http://marriage.about.com/cs/cohabitation/a/cohabseniors.htm
[120] http://www.mcclatchydc.com/news/nation-world/national/article24696883.html

there can be animosities and misunderstandings. Enjoy the romance and companionship but protect yourself and your estate.

In **summary**, here are some issues to consider:

These are things I can do to interact with my spouse when I retire:	1. 2. 3. 4. 5.
These are things my spouse can do to interact with me.	1. 2. 3. 4. 5.
I would accept a Boomerang child (young adult) back into my home	Yes No
If my answer to the above were "Yes", I would want these financial arrangements:	1. 2. 3. 4. 5.
If my answer to the above were "Yes", I would want these social guidelines:	1. 2. 3. 4. 5.
I would take a grandchild into my house if conditions warranted it.	Yes No

If my answer to the above were "Yes", I would cope by doing these things.	1. 2. 3. 4. 5.
If my answer to the above were "Yes", I would use these guidelines in raising the child.	1. 2. 3. 4. 5.
I might cohabit with a partner if I lost my spouse.	Yes No
If my answer to the above were "Yes", I would want these financial arrangements:	1. 2. 3. 4. 5.
If my answer to the above were "Yes", I would protect my children through these actions.	1. 2. 3. 4. 5.

Chapter Seven

What are lifestyle options?

Where will you live in retirement? Are you going to stay in the same house? Are you going to move? Will you move within the same city or to another state?

> *A wise person once told us: "You cannot follow your children around to be near them. You will never know where they will end up."*

A good rule of thumb when you retire is: Do not move right away. Even if you contemplate a move, do not do it within the first six months or even a year. Research carefully so you will know the region to which you are moving and why you want to move there. If you are married, be certain your spouse is as keen on the move, without pressure or coercion.

Moving. There are good reasons to move after you retire. You have been in a work mode for years. Everything about the house facilitates going to work. It might have been close to your job or commute station. It might have been near people who worked at the same place. Maybe you lived there out of habit. Now you can rethink the validity of the house or where you reside and how it functions as a retirement home.

Another reason to move is your house is too big. You simply do not need the space. City dwellers live in small spaces but suburbanites prefer larger dwellings. Perhaps the landscaping is more than you need. You might be in a hot real estate market and the opportunity to sell would give you cash to support retirement, even if you purchase another house or condo. Perhaps the utilities and property taxes have escalated far more than you care to pay.

> *As J. said: "We changed where we live in retirement because I wanted to be able to see the sky again. We lived in Georgia for thirty years. The second home we had there was primarily built with our own labor. We*

lived there for twenty-three years and never ceased working on the structure or the surrounding twelve acres of woods. The trees were so dense that I could not see the sky from inside the house. The walls and ceiling were totally covered with cedar paneling that made the inside of the house dark. I grew up in the wide-open spaces of Kansas and I did not want to spend the remainder of my life closed in by darkness. I felt that as long as we lived on that piece of land that we would never be free of the hard physical work required to maintain it. I also felt that if we did not move when D. retired that we would never move. D. did not want to leave our home but he reasoned that during our marriage I had followed him to where his work led. Now it was my turn to have some choice in deciding where we would live."

There are as many reasons to move when you retire as there are people retiring. But there are some good reasons not to move. To be near the rest of your family is often cited, whether family is children, siblings or even parents. This is often a guilt-driven reason for moving. Are you going to be happier in retirement because you are closer to these people? If yes, then consider it.

It is important to consider the consequences of moving to another state. Some retirees save on taxes. Others do it because of sunshine. A move to an unknown place can be a huge risk. It is better to travel there and rent a house for 3-6 months before you actually move. And the questions to ask: What is the cost of living? How will moving out-of-state impact retirement benefits? Medical benefits? Your health? Lifestyle? Your relationship with your spouse or partner? The desire to fulfill retirement goals and dreams?

A different dwelling can be a spark in retirement. It forces you to think differently because work habits are not embedded. Similarly, a new place can provide a different climate and new retirement opportunities, even part-time employment. Retirees may want to get away from congestion and high housing prices. Selling a home in a high-end market allows them to purchase a new home in a cheaper market, using the $500,000 capital gains exclusion on the Federal tax return. [121] This is the amount excluded for a married couple that has lived in their home for at least 2 of the last 5 years. This is a huge bonus. Income tax is not deferred; it is totally excluded. If you paid $150,000 for your home and it is now worth $650,000 (married filing jointly), you do not pay any capital gains tax when you sell. The $650,000 represents a return of the original $150,000 (your basis) plus $500,000 gain, neither of which is taxed. This can be repeated every 2 years if you live in your next house that long and have a gain.

Popular States. What are the most popular states for retirees? The exodus is from the largest urban regions, particularly California, the Midwest and Eastern states. [122] Retirees use their home equity in high-priced markets to fund their retirement by moving to places where the price of housing can be half as much. In Alaska, the growth in senior population was 58%, in Nevada, 53%, and in Arizona, 37% between 2000 and 2011, [123] partially because of lower cost housing. In addition to cheaper housing, retirees seek four-season locations and return to places similar to or where they grew up. Many want to be rid of urban congestion, but, nonetheless, want to be within a few hours of large cities. Their families might be there and top medical facilities are available. In addition, there are more opportunities for part-time work.

> *W. and L. did it this way: "We had planned and prepared for five years to retire. W. wanted to travel. We had decided that traveling on a sailboat would be an exciting and economical way to see the world. After sailing for five years, we looked extensively for our next house. We compiled parameters we used to make an educated and deliberate decision. Our first choice was California where the bulk of W.'s family is but the cost of housing had escalated to a level, which we did not want to pay. We looked in Florida and Texas. We ended up in*

---

[121] https://www.irs.gov/taxtopics/tc701.html
[122] http://www.bankrate.com/finance/retirement/best-places-retire-how-state-ranks.aspx
[123] *Ibid.*

Arizona where we got the most for our money. L. liked the "active" part of what their choice was touted to be, an "active adult retirement resort community."

Tax Consequences. The impact of taxes, whether on personal income, property or estates is also important. [124] Each state has its own rules on residency as well as exclusion of retirement income earned out-of-state. [125] There are numerous sources for researching this issue. [126] Regardless where you move, do an investigation by contacting the taxing agencies in that state to calculate the advantages and disadvantages. Emotion is important but retirement security depends on financial planning. Tax knowledge is part of it.

New Home Features. Part of the reason for moving is to downsize. [127] In a world where everything is supersized, downsizing seems incompatible to the American mentality. That is because families outgrow one home and move to a larger one. This can occur several times in a family's life cycle. In retirement, the growth is done. It is time to think smaller. A house that is too big to clean, repair and maintain and on which property tax and insurance are expensive is not a boon to comfortable retirement.

Pre-retirees should look for a different house five years after they become empty nesters. What they want is not necessarily a smaller house, since family and friends may visit. Rather, they want a house with amenities and living space on one level, without stairs and basements. The arrangement of space and equipment is important, including open floor plans, wide hallways, and lever-operated doors. Flat thresholds, pocket doors and crank-open windows are important. Senior amenities that are important, should one become wheel chair dependent, include:

---

[124] http://money.cnn.com/2013/06/18/pf/taxes/state-tax/

[125] http://taxfoundation.org/article/state-and-local-sales-tax-rates-2015

[126] https://turbotax.intuit.com/tax-tools/tax-tips/Taxes-101/States-with-the-Highest-and-Lowest-Taxes/INF23232.html

[127] http://www.wsj.com/articles/SB10001424052702303448204579338571140024380

- Wide doors

- Showers, rather than bathtubs

- Railings in shower and toilet areas

- Comfort level toilets and bathroom counters (pedestal vanities)

- Ample lighting in all areas including hallways

- Ample heating (so space heaters are not used)

- Walk-in closets without thresholds

- No steps from garage to house or entryway to house

- Low pile carpeting

- Non-slick floors (tile, hardwood, linoleum, cork)

- Convenient and logical arrangement of light switches

- Large and simple dials on appliances

- Ample power outlets so extension cords are not needed

- Roll out shelves on cabinets

Adult Communities. Age-based retirement communities have appeal to many retirees. These homes, which are often town homes on small lots or condominiums, are often built adjacent to golf courses with club and craft houses. Most have tennis and pickleball courts, fitness centers, swimming pools and other recreational facilities.

Real estate marketers appeal to buyers with an "active-adult community" label instead of "retirement community". There is typically an age restriction for living there, that is, one member of the household must be 55 or more and no one under 19 can live there. To retain its age restriction under Federal guidelines, 80% of households must comply with these rules.[128]

The advantage of an active-adult community is the social life that accompanies. One is buying a lifestyle and socio-economic strata as much as a house. [129] Although active-adult communities provide instant networking and a circle of friends, there are

---

[128] https://en.wikipedia.org/wiki/Age-restricted_community

[129] http://www.seniorliving.org/retirement/55plus-communities/

downsides. Since there is an age restriction, your home as an investment no longer appeals to any buyer. The Conditions, Covenants and Restrictions (CCRs) are usually strict and fully enforced. Although this maintains property value, it can inhibit one's quiet enjoyment of the property if color of a house, a parked car or landscaping is out of compliance. The booming market for these communities should never be an inhibitor for disposing of the property upon one's move to assisted living or death. CCRs must always be fully disclosed before one purchases or sells.

"So the decision was made", said D. " We would move, but I refused to leave our home for any place east of the Mississippi. That was fine with J. She loves the big sky country. Her research had brought us to Arizona, which satisfied both of us. We collaborated mightily on selecting and tailoring the house model, and shopping for all of its accessories and furnishings. Housekeeping and yard work were not important. This was a low maintenance home, wasn't it? That is why we came here, wasn't it? J. wanted our time to be OUR time, at home, together, sharing dreams and sharing work, building our new life. The world outside our property lines could be held at bay for the time being. "

Manufactured Homes. Some adult communities combine manufactured homes and recreational vehicles. A manufactured home, as the name implies, is factory built and assembled. It is then moved to a site and installed on a foundation. There is mobility to these residences since they are built without knowledge of where they will ultimately be placed. But once placed, they seldom are moved. Nonetheless, they are built according to a Federal code, which is overseen by the Department of Housing and Urban Development (HUD), [130] rather than state and local building codes. Most manufacturers are regional and therefore cognizant of local code when the home is to be delivered and installed.

---

[130] http://portal.hud.gov/hudportal/HUD?src=/program_offices/housing/ramh/mhs/faq

The statistics on manufactured homes are ostensible. Seventeen million families live in them. [131] Manufactured homes are lower in cost than site-built homes, averaging $45.41 (2014) per square foot compared to almost double for site-build homes. [132] This does not include the land. Owners of manufactured homes often rent the space on which the home is placed, lowering cost of ownership since there is no property tax to pay. Many states, however, do levy a personal property or use tax on the structure.

Manufactured home parks may include many of the amenities associated with active-adult communities, including clubhouses, golf courses and recreational activities. Living space in one's unit and lot size are typically small but so are the costs to purchase and maintain.

The greatest downside to manufactured homes, which have improved since the HUD code was established in 1976, is sustaining value. They deteriorate quicker than a site-built house. Unless the land on which they are placed is owned, the unit will depreciate much like an automobile. Although most units are never moved, there still is the stigma of "mobility" that makes it difficult to obtain a conforming mortgage. Those units, which are placed on leased land, are financed as unsecured personal loans, with a higher interest rate than conventional mortgages. Although the market for manufactured homes was 20% of all homes in 1998, it had declined to 7.4% by 2012. [133]

Because many people purchase a manufactured home fully furnished, with little down, if anything, equity does not grow quickly. The default rate is four times higher than site-built homes. To this downside must be added their vulnerability to hurricanes, particularly in Southern states. Many manufactured homes are in parks where the population is stagnant. This means there are pools of the "very old" living in near-

---

131

http://cfed.org/programs/innovations_manufactured_homes/about_manufactured_housing/facts_about_manufactured_housing/
[132] http://www.census.gov/construction/mhs/pdf/sitebuiltvsmh.pdf
[133] http://www.fanniemae.com/resources/file/research/datanotes/pdf/housing-insights-0613.pdf

poverty conditions. Nonetheless, manufactured housing will continue to be a major force in low-cost affordable housing for retirees.

Recreational Vehicles (RV) and Full-timing. Some retirees sell all their real estate and downsize to a recreational vehicle, [134] totally eschewing on-site life for a continuous change of scenery and climate. A recreational vehicle can be a travel trailer, including the fifth-wheel, which is towed by an automobile or pickup truck. It can be a self-contained van (Class B), a bus-type motor home (Class A), or a large truck with a living unit on its back frame and over the cab (Class C). All three are vehicles in which you live yet can move under their own power. It is difficult to estimate how many Americans live permanently in one of these devices. One source claims over one million, [135] another, only 250,000.[136] It is hard to pin down statistics when owners and users are mobile. Many owners still work but move frequently because of their jobs (construction workers, highway engineers, inspectors). Many are retirees.

The actual cost of an RV varies widely. One can purchase a used trailer for less than $5,000 while a high-line Class A motor home can cost over $2,000,000. They can be purchased new and used, the latter having an advantage because of the steep depreciation curve on new units.

> *J. was ready to sell the big house and buy a 40-foot Class A motor home. No more community. No more yard work. The best view would be from wherever they parked it. They could summer in Maine and the Maritime Provinces and gradually work their way down to Florida, possibly California or Texas for the winter. K. was more practical. "Let's rent a small RV for a month and see how it goes. I'm not ready to sell nor am I ready to put everything in storage. What if we do not like the RV*

---

[134] http://www.rv-coach.com/rv_types.html

[135] http://www.bbc.com/news/magazine-24135022

[136] http://sangeo-travels.blogspot.com/2011/04/how-many-people-live-full-time-in-rv.html

lifestyle? What if we feel insecure without a place to which we can return? What if we cannot handle a big rig?"

Where will you park your RV? Almost anywhere you want. With portable units, you can "boondock" or "dry camp". RVs have fresh water tanks as well as holding tanks for waste water (grey from sinks and shower and black from the toilet). There are on-board generators, storage batteries and solar panels to supply power. You are independent, as long as you park where it is legal and not just in any parking lot.

If you want amenities, you can rent a space (or even buy one) in the numerous RV parks across the entire country as well as Canada and Mexico, costing anywhere from $10 to over $100 a night. Some parks are limited to high-end vehicles of a certain elegance, length and vintage. Regardless what you drive and live in, there is camaraderie among RVers that is unequalled among any other group of people: the love of following the open road, changing scenery and seeking the sun. The costs associated with full timing are proportional to the original investment of your unit, how far you travel and where you park it. It can be as expensive as owning a big city condominium or much less.

The downside, however, is that you will probably not fulltime forever. Eventually, you may want to settle in a site-built house. If you stay out of the housing market too long, you may find re-entry in the area you choose financially prohibitive. When you own a home, even if you RV part- or fulltime, your equity continues to grow. An alternative, of course, is eventually to sell your RV and rent an apartment or move to assisted-living.

In **summary**, your lifestyle options in retirement are numerous. Complete this chart as summary to the issues presented in this chapter:

I plan to move right before or after I retire.	
	Yes No

If "no", these are the reasons I will stay in my house.	1. 2. 3. 4. 5.
If "yes", these are reasons I want to move.	1. 2. 3. 4. 5.
These are geographical areas to which I would consider moving.	1. 2. 3. 4. 5.
I have investigated the tax consequences of these moves.	Yes No
If I am downsizing, I want these amenities in my new house.	1. 2. 3. 4. 5.
I want these amenities in the development or location I choose.	1. 2. 3. 4. 5.
I would consider a move to an active-adult community.	Yes No
I would consider buying a manufactured home.	Yes No

I would consider purchasing an RV and full timing.	Yes No

Chapter Eight

What are you going to do with all the stuff?

You are ready to move to something smaller and more manageable. What are you going to do with all of your stuff?

> *For L., it was efficient but not easy: "We sold our house to friends six months before we moved, rented it back, and I took that time to dispose of everything. I made piles for the church auction, for an antique store, for each child, for the dump, and finally for Arizona. The hardest items to get rid of were the books in our floor to ceiling library. But that was a good lesson. Today, I never keep a book after I've read it."*

Your family will give you strife about moving. They love the big old house where they grew up. Your Boomerang daughter has enjoyed the comforts of home and your cooking for two years after graduating college. She does not want to find and pay for her own . Your son, daughter-in-law and their two kids enjoy the holidays in the big house. But they do not have to pay the taxes, utilities and upkeep. And they enjoy going to the attic and looking through the things that you have saved since childhood. But they never take those things back to their house. It is fine for you to keep it. They do not want it in their lives, except when they visit.

It is time for the stuff to go. Children move ahead in their lives but somehow want Mom and Dad to remain the same in the same house with the same stuff.

Downsizing. Downsizing should never be done in a hurry. When it is, there is a tendency to throw too much away or too little. You need a strategic plan how to sort, make decisions, save for moving or divesting. When you move from a 3600 square foot two-story to a 1800 sq. foot town home, you need to get rid of 50% of what you own, whether furniture, clothes, equipment, or memorabilia. [137]

Furniture. A good starting place is furniture. Ask yourself: How many bedrooms in the new place? Will the old beds fit? Will you use a bedroom for an office? How does your current living or family room furniture fit in the new house? Are there pieces you are not using now that will not be used in a new environment? What is built-in?

If the move is long and your furniture old, divest of all and begin anew, if there is no sentimental value. The cost of moving is likely more than the old furniture is worth. Do not be tempted to store furniture. If you do not have room for it in a new house when you first move, it is doubtful you will later.

> *The antique wardrobe and dressers had been in the family for two generations. M. knew they would not fit into a beachfront condo in California, but there was such sentimental value. She moved them anyway at great cost and found they did not fit. Fortunately, an antique dealer in Los Angeles saw their value and took them off her hands. But he paid her less than it cost to ship them from Minnesota.*

Clothes. If you are moving to a warmer climate, winter coats may no longer be needed. Clothes from your job, dress suits, neckties and starched shirts, are not going to be worn. If you have not used it in the past year, it goes out. One or two professional outfits and lots of casual clothes will be de rigueur in retirement. Styles and fabrics change over time. A fresh and new look in retirement is an exciting objective.

Memorabilia. Memorabilia is a sentimental issue. You divest of your son's first grade painting or your daughter's first 4-H blue ribbon by passing them to your children. If they do not want them, out they go. The memory is not lost just because the memorabilia

---

[137] http://www.styleathome.com/homes/real-estate/top-10-tips-for-downsizing/a/308

is in the trashcan. Photos are sorted and shared with family members. Keep the most important ones, which are probably 10% of what you have. If you keep more, scan and put them on computer. Photos that have not been arranged in albums by the time you retire will probably not be arranged later. Scrapbooking is a tedious job with few rewards. Photos are better shared on FaceBook, not a family album.

This is true for family treasures and heirlooms. What you do not want, give first right of refusal to your children, second to your relatives and third to your friends. Whatever you do, do fairly, thoroughly and definitely.

Electronic Equipment. Electronic equipment, radios, TVs, recorders, computers and peripherals collect in all houses. Keep the newest, the most advanced. Electronic equipment becomes better and less expensive each year. Why move a TV set that is ten years old?

> *G. loved his 52-inch projection TV. He had watched six Super Bowls on it and he enjoyed its ease of operation. But L. thought they should donate it to a charity and not move something that big clear across the country. They could buy a flat-screen TV when they resettled in their new state, which had a lower sales tax rate. G. said: "I paid almost $5000 for that set and it is still good." She answered: "And you have used it for over six years. That comes out to $2.25 a day! Let it go!"*

Make the garage the "out" place. Whatever is not moving goes to the garage. Family and friends can walk through and make selections. The sorting should take no longer than a week. If it takes more time, you begin to move items from the garage back into your house. Pretty soon, the garage is bare. When in doubt, throw it out. What you do not see, you will not miss. In less than a year in a new environment, you will forget you ever owned it.

Dishes and silver you will probably keep, unless you have two or more sets. Retirement entertainment is casual so do not keep more than 12 place settings. If you plan to serve larger groups, cater your event or use fancy paper plates. Keep what is essential; divest of the rest.

Garage Sales. Your garage is full. What are you going to do with it? Are there items of value? If your neighborhood allows, have a three-day garage sale. If you can arrange a sale the same day others in the neighborhood have one, traffic will be heavier and you will move more items. [138]

Who comes to garage sales? Some are treasure hunters, looking for the low-priced antique or rare painting. Others purchase your stuff and resell it at their own garage sale or a swap meet for more money. There are low-income people who cannot afford to pay retail prices who will traffic your garage sale. There are people looking for an incredible bargain. Finally, there are the mere curious.

You may need a permit from the homeowners' association, city or county. Most urban areas and many housing developments have rules on garage sales, such as having a permit at least seventy-two hours before the event. The sale itself may only be on consecutive days. Goods must be household items, not newly purchased merchandise. All items must be in the garage or patio. There may be limits on the number of signs and where they can be posted. It is also illegal to sell recalled items. It is good to post notification on designated websites. [139]

Price everything in the garage with tags. Do not be afraid to haggle. Customers expect it and you are merely selling stuff, not your pride or self-esteem. If an item is in excellent shape (like new), price it at half its original value. If it is not, price it between 10-25% of

---

[138] http://www.wcpo.com/money/consumer/dont-waste-your-money/3-secrets-to-a-successful-yard-or-garage-sale
[139] http://www.yardsalesearch.com

its original value. Household items sell best under $2, then $2-5, $5-10, and over $10. Rarely price anything over $50.

Garage sales never return huge amounts of cash, unless you are selling appliances and silver. Price to divest. Lay items out by category on tables and include a table of "free for the taking". Do not extend the sale to the inside of your house. If you have appliances, include a sign that says "available for viewing with owner only". Place ads in the newspaper and position signs where legal, citing place, date and time. Put a sign in front of your driveway.

Even though people may arrive an hour before you intend to begin, do not open early. It is not fair to those who read your ad and complied. Have a cash box with at least $50 in small denominations and coins. Alert your neighbors and solicit help from them as well as your family. Do not take checks without guarantee cards. Run the sale for two days and then discount everything on the third day. If anything remains, call a charitable organization to pick up as a donation.

The garage sale is a way of seeing your neighbors and announcing you are downsizing and moving on. It is not the easiest way to get rid of material goods. In addition, you should check your homeowner's insurance policy to be certain you are covered should someone be injured during the sale. Policies typically cover a garage sale if it is a one-time event and you are doing it yourself. If you cannot bear the trauma, there are professionals who will do it, pricing items at what the market will bear. Their brokerage is typically 1/3 of receipts. It is also possible to call a thrift pick-up truck and donate all your cast-offs to charity. You can write-off up to $500 on your income tax for the year under charitable giving. [140] If something is worth more, you need to have a special form completed by an appraiser for income tax purposes. Unless you badly need the cash, this is a sane way to divest.

---

[140] http://www.marketwatch.com/story/7-tax-rules-that-apply-to-noncash-charitable-donations-2015-02-16

They had dreaded the notion of a garage sale. The neighbors would surely think they needed the money in order to retire, which was not true. But L. and R. had lots of things they did not want to move upstate to their new condo. The spinet piano was worth $1500. They decided to donate all the household goods to a local charity for resale and the piano to the community college. The college provided them an official appraisal of $1500, which they could then take off on Form 8283 of their federal income tax. The non-cash donation of $500 with the spinet would save them about $800 in income tax for the year.

Consignment. If the household goods are worth more, use consignment. [141] It may take more time than three days of a garage sale and not return any more. Check the shop to see how items are displayed and if your goods are compatible with what the store displays. Check how much traffic the location has. Inventory valuables that you consign, including their condition, so that if they are damaged, the store takes responsibility. All consignments should be in writing, specifying the profit split and timetable for retrieval.

You can also divest of equipment and household items on eBay [142] and Craig's List. [143] You open an account and post your items by price and category. The brokerage fee is low. Craig's List is a local operation but eBay is national. There are guidelines to follow with both services, and the timeline is not necessarily efficient for quick disposal.

In **summary**, complete this chart to prepare for downsizing.

I will downsize my household when I move.	Yes No

---

[141] https://en.wikipedia.org/wiki/Consignment
[142] http://www.ebay.com/gds/What-exactly-is-eBay-Consignment-/10000000015164697/g.html
[143] https://www.craigslist.org/about/sites

If "yes", these are categories of items to divest.	1. 2. 3. 4. 5.
These are items I will give to family and friends.	1. 2. 3. 4. 5.
I will hold a garage sale.	Yes No (If "no", skip next 3 items)
I will need a permit.	Yes No
My homeowner's policy covers the event.	Yes No
My timeline will be:	1. Prepare, sort and price 2. Hold sale 3. Call charity
I will place the goods on consignment	Yes No (If "no", skip next item)
Possible stores are:	1. 2. 3. 4.
I will donate some items to charitable groups	Yes No
These groups are	1. 2. 3. 4.

I will have downsized what I will not move by (time)	

Chapter Nine

How can you live on the cheap?

S. did not like to consider herself cheap. She was thrifty. She was frugal. On trips to the grocery store, she was armed with coupons. She always asked for the senior discount when she had her hair done. She never bought a household good or an item of clothing that was not on sale. She would drive five extra miles to save three cents per gallon of gasoline. Few of her friends or neighbors knew it, but she and her husband had a net worth of over $2,500,000.

You may not need to, but can you live on the cheap? People who are frugal often accumulate the most wealth. If you retired with 70%, 100% or 130% of pre-retirement income, you probably have lived on the cheap. That does not mean you are cheap. It means you have spent less than you earned. In retirement, you can now polish these bargain-seeking skills into a perfected art form.

Price Discrimination. Price discrimination [144] works to the advantage of anyone who has time to do things other than during normal business hours. Some retirees call it a "senior discount", [145] thinking it is a largesse they deserve because they are old or poor. Nothing is further from the truth. Price discrimination is a way a business shifts demand for a product or service from high demand times to periods when demand is low.

Restaurants are a good example. Early in the evening, there are few customers. [146] Nonetheless, if the restaurant is open, it needs a chef, servers and clean-up crew whether they are busy or not. To shift demand from a later hour, 7 p.m for example, when more patrons begin to dine, the restaurant offers "senior" meals or "sunset" meals at discount

---

[144] http://www.investopedia.com/terms/p/price_discrimination.asp
[145] https://www.quora.com/Why-do-stores-give-senior-citizen-discounts
[146] https://en.wikipedia.org/wiki/Early_bird_dinner

to encourage people to dine earlier. Although the price of the meal is less than it would be at a later hour, the fixed costs associated with staffing are met. Trade volume ends up being slightly higher. An astute retiree will take advantage of these discounts, which are not "senior" discounts at all, but a discount for eating earlier. Anyone can participate. The business keeps revenue flowing even though demand is lower.

The same scenario occurs in movie theatres. Demand is lower at matinees but costs of staffing and running the film remain the same. Therefore the noon matinee is discounted, encouraging retirees or anyone to attend earlier in the day

There are numerous examples of price discrimination of which retirees can take advantage. Most are services, not consumer products. If one were able to buy a car at discount in the morning, there would be nothing to prevent the buyer from selling the car in the afternoon for more money. Price discrimination applies to restaurants, movie theatres, happy hours at bars, mid-week cruises, haircuts, mid-week discounts on hotel rooms and airline tickets with Tuesday, Wednesday or Saturday departures/arrivals. [147] We are advantaged by these discounts, not because we are old and deserve them, but, rather, because it is good business practice to shift demand.

Automobile and house insurance use price discrimination too. Premiums are based on one's driving record and the number of claims filed. Safer drivers and homeowners with no claims have lower premiums. Auto insurers provide a lower premium for driving fewer miles a year, usually under 7,500. [148] This is from lower risk, not from being older, and anyone who drives fewer miles is eligible. It is not a senior discount.

Retires can take advantage of price discrimination by eating out earlier, attending matinee shows and concerts as well as notifying one's insurance agent if he or she drives fewer miles per year.

---

[147] http://www.farecompare.com/travel-advice/tips-from-air-travel-insiders/#/
[148] http://www.post-gazette.com/business/money/2015/05/27/There-are-lots-of-car-insurance-discounts-out-there-if-you-ask/stories/201505210008

F. always told his friends they attended the noon matinee and got discount tickets because they were seniors and had earned a bargain. Finally, one of his friends told him it had nothing to do with being old. The theatre managers were shifting demand to a time of day when most people worked and were not able to attend. He said to F.: "Try getting a senior discount at the 7 p.m. showing on Saturday night!"

Dining Out. Dining out is an excellent way to demonstrate how to live on the cheap. If a meal out is an infrequent celebration, go all the way. But if you dine out once or twice a week, economize on the tab. If you drink cocktails, have them in the adjacent bar during "happy hour". Drinks may be half-price then. If you are having the drink with dinner, carry it into your restaurant table with you from the bar, rather than ordering from your server. Drink regular tap water with dinner. It is better for you and it is free.

Order from the sunset meal menu. It is the same food that appears on the regular menu later in the evening, possibly in smaller portions. Avoid ordering ala carte but look for menu items that include a salad with your entrée. Skip the appetizer and check on specials. They may be less expensive. If you and your partner are not big eaters, split an entrée and order an extra house salad. If you have wine with dinner, eschew the bottle and order a half-carafe of house wine. Skip dessert, coffee and after-dinner drink too. These add-ons can more than double the bill you pay for the dinner alone. Regardless whether your tab is $30 or $90, you have the same service, entrée and ambience. This is basic cost-benefit analysis.

Buying and Selling Cars. There are interesting ways to purchase an auto on the cheap. Never purchase because you need a car but because it makes economic sense to divest of an old auto. Many couples do not need two cars in retirement. Divesting of one provides cash and saves on insurance.

Purchasing a new auto means doing research on models and features. An Internet search by manufacturer will reveal rebate offers. Newspaper ads will show which dealers are offering in-house rebates. Many times, you will be able to take advantage of both. You must be flexible on the color of the car as well as amenities already installed. Contact more than one dealer for the best deal. It is always inadvisable to have the dealer add options. These always add undue expense.

When is the best time to buy a car? [149] It used to be September or October when new models appeared. With new models coming out all year, the autumn advantage has evaporated. An effective time of the month to purchase an auto is the last few days. Dealers try to meet quota and move inventory. Saturday morning is good, too, since dealers like to build momentum into the weekend. Many times, the best deals occur on the last day of the month.

If you are married or partnered, one household member should shop for the car. Car salesmen are skilled in playing off emotions and feelings they sense from couples as well as picking up preferences and enthusiasm for making a deal. Individually, find the car you want and determine the lowest price the dealer wants. After leaving, check the dealer's price on the Internet. At this point, the second member of the household goes to the dealership, announcing him or herself as the spouse. On a spreadsheet, the second person has the exact price you are willing to pay for the car. Without discussion, other than "This is what we will pay for the car", the second household member leaves. There is little doubt that before the day is out (if it is the end of the month), the dealer's final offer will be closer to yours. Do not be intimidated by the process and be willing to walk away from a deal that is not right for you, even when you love the car. You do not need the car, you want it.

R. and T. made the mistake of shopping for a new car together. She really wanted a red coupe and he wanted a four-door. Although the price of the sporty coupe was higher than the sedan, the sales person

_____

[149] http://www.ehow.com/facts_5002301_best-time-buy-new-car.html

114

was clever in dropping comments like: "Your spouse is going to be happier with this little coupe." "It really has style. Just think what your friends will say when you drive by. There was another couple just here who had a strong interest in that red coupe." They bought the coupe and paid a higher price.

Arrange financing before the search. Dealer financing will cost more. If you pay cash, you are free to haggle, rather than be swayed by: "How much would you like your monthly payments to be?" of the salesperson. The bottom line is always the price of the car, not the monthly payment. Do not overlook the possibility of leasing a car with little down. It frees up cash and there are good deals for low-mileage drivers.

How do you sell your old car? [150] Good, clean used cars are easy to sell. The car should be detailed. Then place an ad, checking and printing blue book value.[151] Price it $500 more than what you will accept. When buyers come, let them drive it with you in the passenger's seat. If you suspect something is adverse when a person calls or comes to the house, say the car is unavailable. Always carry a cell phone and alert your partner where you are going. Once a buyer is found, require a cash deposit or cashier's check of at least 5% to hold it. Determine when and where the total selling price will be delivered, such as a bank or credit union, and meet there to hand over notarized title and vehicle when you receive the full selling price as cash or cashier's check.

Thrifting. Why pay retail when there are second-hand consumer goods available? Thrifting is the answer. [152] Second-hand autos and motor homes of recent vintage and low mileage are good buys, particularly if still under manufacturer's warranty. Household appliances, however, are rarely good items to buy used. The price of new and the quality it represents probably outweigh dealing with equipment that someone else has

---

[150] http://www.wikihow.com/Sell-Your-Car-Privately
[151] http://www.kbb.com
[152] http://www.wisebread.com/10-things-to-look-for-every-time-you-visit-a-thrift-store

sold because it had a problem. [153]   Other than outward appearance, which tells little, there is not much to distinguish a good used appliance from a worn out one.

Furniture and clothing, however, are different. People divest because their tastes change, they re-decorate, they gain weight, or a button is missing. Both furniture and clothing have high mark-up in retail stores. They can be purchased for less than half the original cost when used. What you see usually determines whether it is good or not. And the investment, particularly with clothes, is so low that the decision is not inexorable.

Furniture. Used furniture is best purchased from private parties who advertise in the newspaper, either to sell one or two pieces or part of downsizing a house or an estate sale. You have to know what you are looking for and how it will integrate into your new house. [154] Always measure the space in your house to fill and take samples of carpet, tile or colors from present pieces of furniture, as well as a tape measure, before you begin the search. A wonderful buy may not fit in your home. With used furniture, you have to make a fast decision, since others may be waiting in line to buy the same piece.

Nonetheless, there are features to look for in furniture, whether new or used. [155] What materials are used? Solid hardwood, softwood or particleboard? Solid grain, veneer or a simulated product? How is the wood joined? Tongue and groove, screws or glue? Is the finish even and deep or are there bubbles and brush strokes? Are cushions nicely detailed with solid buttons, all attached? Are they evenly plumped or sagging with spring indentations? Is the furniture clean and does it appear to have been treated with care? Fabrics can be cleaned and recovered, if the framework is quality. Used furniture, to be a bargain, must show quality and care. Otherwise, buy new. Good furniture choices come from effective planning and decisioning and will therefore serve you for a period of time.

---

[153] http://www.standardtvandappliance.com/4-tips-on-buying-used-appliances/
[154] http://freshome.com/2010/09/17/20-tips-for-buying-second-hand-furniture/
[155] http://freshome.com/2008/05/27/5-useful-tips-for-buying-used-furniture/

Clothing. Why pay retail for good clothing? You do not need much in retirement and it is fun to haunt the thrift shops for bargains. [156] With used clothing, women fare better than men. Women divest of clothes for a variety of reasons: it does not fit; it is the wrong color; it needs repair; it does not make her feel good. Men divest of clothes, for one reason: it is worn out. Consequently, the good buys in thrift stores are for women, much more than for men.

It is important to know labels when thrifting. [157] If it does not have a label, it could be homemade or a second. Look for the right size, color, fit, style, fabric and condition. Buttons can be replaced and rips in seams repaired. But a snagged fabric or a spot that may prove to be permanent are not worth the bother. Merchandise is sold "as is". Look the garment over thoroughly before purchasing. Finally, price is an issue. If the price is near retail, buy new.

> *J. was always well dressed. Whether resort wear for the golf course, slacks and sweater for card games or formal wear for holiday parties, she never failed to be turned out with haute couture. Her friends assumed she spent a fortune on clothes, most of which were designer labels. In reality, the stunning cocktail dress she wore to the last party had been purchased at a trendy thrift shop in the city for $15 on "senior day".* The hem had been slightly pulled, but she repaired it in 10 minutes.*
>
> **Low demand day*

Thrifting allows you to buy "one of a kind", rather than look for your size among racks of identical outfits. Vintage clothes are also an attraction. [158] There is great pleasure and pride in putting together a designer outfit at minimal cost. Inventory in thrift stores turns

---

[156] http://www.wikihow.com/Shop-Well-for-Clothes-in-a-Thrift-Store
[157] http://www.dailyfinance.com/2008/01/25/to-thrift-or-not-to-thrift-check-your-labels-for-quality/
[158] http://sammydvintage.com/thrifting/vintage-clothing-labels-tips/

over quickly, so a favorite outlet might have what you want the day after you looked. And it will not be there the next day when you come back, so there is little chance to ponder your decision. At the reduced prices of thrift stores, most garments are not investments that will render you insolvent, should you make a wrong decision. [159] You can always donate your mistakes back to the same thrift shop.

In **summary,** complete this chart to assess how to live frugally:

These are examples of price discrimination in my community among merchants of which I can take advantage to spend less money	1. 2, 3. 4. 5.
The last time I ate in a restaurant, these are ala carte items I bought that drove up the price of my bill.	1. 2, 3. 4. 5.
If I were purchasing a new car, I would follow these steps to negotiate an equitable price and deal	1. 2, 3. 4. 5.
If I were selling my own car to a private party, I would follow this strategy	1. 2, 3. 4. 5.

---

[159] http://wholenaturallife.com/2013/03/29/five-tips-for-buying-used-clothing-at-thrift-stores/

If I were buying used furniture, I would follow these guidelines	1.
	2,
	3.
	4.
	5.
If I were buying used clothing, I would follow these guidelines	1.
	2,
	3.
	4.
	5.

Chapter Ten

Should you spend your children's inheritance?

C. and B.'s needs were fully met with pensions and Social Security benefits. They had never tapped into their 401k but knew they would soon, once they turned 70 1/2. What should they do with the extra money? They knew their church could use some of it. C.s' middle son was trying to make a new start after retiring from the military. He was working on an associate degree in computer technology. He could not pick up a job to supplement his military retirement. Should they gift some of their 401k money to him?

Retirement is good. You have downsized and enjoy your new home. Your lifestyle is healthy. You have found worthwhile things to do, including a part-time job. Your new car was an incredible bargain. You dine out twice a week and enjoy good theatre and sporting events. You have been on a two-week cruise and weekend car trips. Your three pools of funds are working for you. You are confident you will not outlive your financial resources. Therefore, should you spend your children's inheritance? Or should you leave them money?

This is not a question one can ever answer. You do not know how long you will live. You are not certain what time and inflation may do to your personal savings, pension and Social Security benefits. And what have you already done for your children and grandchildren? Did you help them purchase a car? A home? Pay college expenses? Finance a big wedding?

Gifting. The greatest inheritance parents and grandparents can endow on offspring is the ability to earn a good living. More young people have some form of higher education, whether community college, trade school or university and graduate school. The rising cost of tuition is deferred through student loans. In 2014-2015, the average price for tuition at a two-year public school was $9,139, at a four-year public institution, $16,482 and at a four-year private school, $34,193. [160] Tuition and fees will only accelerate over time, as they have in the past fifteen years. It is predicted the above figures will be, respectively, $35,700, $102,900 and $355,900 by 2029. [161] Upon completion, your children or grandchildren have debt. The average debt in 2015 for students with a four-year degree was $35,051. [162] And 60% of all aid is in the form of loans. [163] Loans are largely need-based. But with an education, earning potential will be much higher.

For children or grandchildren who have graduated and proven their ability to attend and graduate, you can help pay off loans. At age 70 1/2 (actually, April 1 following the month in which you turn 70 1/2), you must begin withdrawing funds from tax-sheltered accounts, whether an IRA, 401k or 403b. [164] If you are living comfortably on what your personal savings, pension and Social Security provide, the sudden and mandatory withdrawal might trigger an impulse to buy a new sports car or cruise to Indonesia. Think what an outright gift can mean to a child or grandchild to pay off college loans. It is better than a lavish wedding or the down payment on a condominium. Other than pay income tax on your withdrawals, what more would you do with the money?

The government allows outright gifts. The rules are linked among gift taxes, estate taxes and a unified credit. Since exclusions and exceptions apply, your accountant best handles these. In general, you can gift up to $14,000 annually (2014-2016) to an individual without triggering tax. Your spouse can do the same, providing $28,000 to an individual

---

[160] http://www.statisticbrain.com/average-cost-of-college-tuition/
[161] *Ibid.*
[162] http://www.marketwatch.com/story/class-of-2015-has-the-most-student-debt-in-us-history-2015-05-08
[163] *Ibid.,* statisticbrain.com/student-loan-debt-statistics/
[164] https://www.irs.gov/Retirement-Plans/Retirement-Plans-FAQs-regarding-IRAs-Distributions-(Withdrawals)

per year. [165] If you have several children or grandchildren who need help and you can afford it, you can gift $28,000 as a couple to each.

There are exceptions to the $14,000 annual limitation. If the gift is for education expenses, it is not considered a gift. The same is true for health reasons, such as paying for a sister's surgery. Gifts to your spouse do not count, as long as you both are American citizens. Finally, there is no tax on gifting to a political organization. [166]

Another way to provide for college expenses in advance is the 529 plan (Section 529 of the Internal Revenue Code). [167] The 529 is a savings plan for future educational expenses, operated by a state government or a specific education institution. Each state has at least one. Some plans provide a savings pool while others actually guarantee prepaid tuition, regardless of inflation, when the beneficiary begins college.

The donor establishes a tax-deferred plan for the recipient. The funds grow tax-deferred. When the money is distributed to the beneficiary, it is tax-free. This plan is available to anyone, regardless of income level. The donor controls the plan, through the program administrator, until the funds are distributed. The 529 has numerous facets, depending on the sponsoring agency. Although there are limits on investments, there is great flexibility in transferring funds to a different institution should a student decide not to attend the university or college originally specified. If the funds eventually do not go to a beneficiary and are returned to the donor, there are tax consequences and possibly penalties, since it is not a tax-avoidance plan.

---

[165] https://www.irs.gov/Businesses/Small-Businesses-&-Self-Employed/Frequently-Asked-Questions-on-Gift-Taxes
[166] http://www.moneycrashers.com/gift-tax-rate-rules-exclusion-limit/
[167] https://www.irs.gov/uac/529-Plans:-Questions-and-Answers

G. and M. wanted to help their grandchildren with college and had the financial resources to do so. For each of their four grandchildren, they opened a 529 on their sixth birthday, adding money on each subsequent birthday for the next twelve years. Although they paid into the plan within their state, only two of the grandchildren went to the state university. The other two elected out-of-state schools, but the proceeds from the 529s were transferred to their chosen institutions. As each grandchild drew on the funds, there was no income tax.

Estate Tax. The American Taxpayer Relief Act of 2012 changed several procedures on gifts and estates. [168] For 2016, the filing requirements apply to estates $5,450,000 or above. [169] The good news is that 99.5% of estates fall below that amount. A person could leave or give away that amount and not owe federal tax. [170] The bad news is that every state deals with estate, death and inheritance taxes differently [171] and there is no universal rule that applies to all fifty different jurisdictions, since state laws are varied and frequently change. [172] What is presented here refers only to federal tax.

Do not spend your children's inheritance. Give it to them $14,000 per year. If you do not, there may be an estate tax on what is left after you pass on, if your estate is large. Your executor pays the tax after you die on the value of your entire estate, including savings, real and personal property, and life insurance proceeds. It includes the value of some property you might have transferred within three years before you died as well as certain annuities. The only allowable deductions are funeral expenses, debts and the property that is left to your surviving spouse, if any.

---

[168] https://en.wikipedia.org/wiki/American_Taxpayer_Relief_Act_of_2012

[169] https://www.irs.gov/Businesses/Small-Businesses-&-Self-Employed/Estate-Tax

[170] http://www.nolo.com/legal-encyclopedia/federal-gift-estate-law-2013-beyond.html

[171] http://wills.about.com/od/stateestatetaxes/a/stateestatetaxchart.htm

[172] http://wills.about.com/od/stateestatetaxes/fl/2015-State-Death-Tax-Exemption-and-Top-Tax-Rate-Chart.htm

The federal estate tax, when it is applied, is progressive, ranging from 18% to 40%, depending upon the amount over the exemption ($5,450,000 for 2016). In 2015, an estate that exceeded the exemption (which was $5,430,000) by $10,000 would have a tax of $1,800 (18% marginal tax rate) while one that exceeded the exemption by $1,000,001 would have a tax of $400,000.4. (40% marginal tax rate) [173] This is due by your executor nine months after you die.

J. and F. had gifted each of their three children $14,000 ($42,000 total per year) for the last four years. When J. passed away, he had given a total of $168,000 to the children. Since their estate was valued at $3,550,000, there was no estate tax. His exclusion was beneath the $5,450,000 limit. Neither was there any gift tax, since the gifts were always $14,000 to each annually.

The Unified Credit combines the Gift Tax and Estate Tax. [174] It is a lifetime gift and estate tax exclusion. If one gives above $14,000 to any individual, the annual exclusion, the Unified Credit applies. The amount over $14,000 is simply deducted from the Unified Credit. In one year should you gift $25,000 to one individual, you have reduced your Unified Credit by $11,000. For 2015, your estate would not be taxed unless it exceeded $5,419,000 ($5,430,000-$11,000). The federal government expects donors to keep a schedule of gifts so the estate executor can calculate how much remains on the non-taxable portion of the estate.

---

[173] https://www.chernoffdiamond.com/services/private-client-executive-life-insurance/private-client-resources/federal-estate-and-gift-tax-tables/

[174] http://www.forbes.com/sites/deborahljacobs/2014/10/30/irs-raises-limit-on-tax-free-lifetime-gifts-for-2015/

Both members in a marriage have the exclusion, $5,450,000 each for 2016. A surviving partner can use the exclusion not exhausted by his or her deceased spouse [175] as long as the surviving spouse elects "portability" of the deceased spouse's exemption. [176]

T. and L. had owned a small factory that provided components to the airline industry in the Northwest. When they sold the business, their net worth was $11,000,000. Over the past two years, L. had given her only child $50,000 a year, which was $36,000 over the gift tax exclusion, which reduced her estate exclusion for 2015 from $5,430,000 to $5,358,000. Had she passed away in 2015, that amount would have been added to T.'s exclusion, if he elected portability, which was $5,430,000, making his total exclusion now $10,788,000. Had he passed away the same year, the estate tax would have been calculated on the difference between his exclusion and $11,000,000, or $212,000. The marginal tax rate is 32% so the tax would be $67,840, due 9 months after his death.

The question whether you spend your children's inheritance is not fair. If you have the means, the joy of sharing money before you die helps your friends and family while it brings you pleasure. If you save it until you die, it becomes a tax liability for your heirs, if your estate is large. The choice is yours.

L. put it this way: "We have no planned savings for inheritance sake. Our plans are to remain financially independent and leave for our heirs whatever money is remaining after our deaths."

---

[175] http://www.attorneyoffice.com/2014-gift-estate-tax-unified-credit-increased/
[176] http://www.mysanantonio.com/life/life_columnists/paul_premack/article/2015-Estate-Tax-and-Gift-Tax-Exemptions-6015061.php

How to handle this is a balancing act between protecting yourself while minimizing your assets so estate tax is not due when you die. The best laid financial plans, articulated throughout this book, often enrich the taxing agencies when we pass on. If we could plan our deaths, these would never be issues. Since we cannot, we do what is right and judicious, living well while helping others as we are able.

When asked how he monitors finances, D. said: "It's really easy. J. and I just exercise reasonable prudence. We hope to have enough to last our lifetimes. Our ultimate goal would be that the check to the undertaker bounces!"

In **summary,** complete this chart to focus your intents regarding your estate.

My estate is large enough to reduce it by gifting	**Yes No** **(If "no", stop here)**
In the next year, I need to reduce my estate by	$
In the next five years, I need to reduce my estate by	$
These are family members who could benefit from my gifting	1. 2. 3. 4. 5.
These are friends who could benefit from my gifting	1. 2. 3. 4. 5.

These are charities or agencies who could benefit from my gifting	1. 2. 3. 4. 5.

Coda

If you have faithfully traveled through this book and discerned what you can do, what is right for you, what works for you and what you will do, congratulations. It is full of advice, much of which is neither intuitive nor easy to follow. [177] All of us think of ourselves as immortal and that retirement is a long way in the future. It comes much quicker than you can ever imagine. [178] Astute financial and emotional planning is the key to building that successful retirement, while never eschewing the daily needs of our mate, our family and friends as well as ourselves. Relationships, ultimately, are more important than bank accounts, but one needs to develop both consistently. And along the way, there are always roadblocks that prevent a linear approach to planning. [179] In spite of these, if one can move forward, saving money and forgetting it, retirement will be the reward.

Retirement will occur. Although it is not something about which we should obsess, planning for it has a place in one's life, not merely as a possibility, but a real eventuality. It is the hope of the author that this book will assist in your planning for a successful and long retirement.

---

[177] http://www.dol.gov/ebsa/publications/10_ways_to_prepare.html
[178] http://www.investopedia.com/university/retirement/retirement1.asp
[179] http://christianpf.com/reasons-why-people-dont-save-for-retirement/

Acknowledgements

Many people assisted with this book either through reviewing the manuscript at various stages of development or providing life stories, which could be integrated into the ideas and concepts, proffered throughout. The author would like to thank Bill and Judy Peterson, Howie and Nancy Ullrich, Lee and Kathie Quiring, Tom O'Brien, and Shirley O'Brien, all of whom read the manuscript and offered suggestions on content, format, and style. A special thank you is due Steve Przewlocki, financial consultant and investment counselor, for unlocking some financial mysteries and suggesting details to enhance the conceptual flow. Thanks to many retirees who contributed life stories and anecdotes to provide human interest to material which could be very dull without real life people, including Manuel De Leon, Alice Guy, Don and Jody Holliday, Patsy Chase, June Boicourt, Karen and Tim Koch, Gordon Hadley and Nancy Lehnert, Florence Schlesinger, Wally and Leon McKinzie, Joe and Lauchette Low and Evelyn and Ben Bonneprise. Your stories are wonderful because they are true.

The anecdotes and vignettes integrated throughout this book are derived from three sources. Some are actual stories, which were provided by the individuals cited above. Some are based on stories, which were provided by these individuals, and some were created to illustrate a point or to enhance a concept.

Special thanks is due to Margaret Groves, fellow RVer, neighbor at Pacific Shores Motor Coach Resort in Newport, Oregon and professional editor, who did a meticulous job in reading the manuscript, finding even the smallest errors and suggesting corrections.

Not to be overlooked! The title: It's Monday Morning: "There Are People in My Office Working . . . and I'm Not One of Them" was coined by my spouse, Shirley. This is what she said the first Monday after she retired.

Appendix 1

Scenarios for Withdrawing Interest and Principal on $200,000

over 25 Years at Various Interest Rates

Year	Interest Rate	Principal Drawn Out	Interest	Total per Year	Total per Month	Principal Value at End Of Year
	2%					
1	2%	$8,000	$4,000	$12,000	$1,000	$192,000
2	2%	$8,000	$3,840	$11,840	$987	$186,000
5	2%	$8,000	$3,200	$11,200	$933	$160,000
7	2%	$8,000	$2,880	$10,880	$907	$144,000
10	2%	$8,000	$2,400	$10,400	$867	$120,000
20	2%	$8,000	$800	$8,800	$733	$40,000
25	2%	$8,000	$160	$8,160	$680	$0
	3%					
1	3%	$8,000	$6,000	$14,000	$1,167	$192,000
2	3%	$8,000	$5,760	$13,760	$1,147	$186,000
5	3%	$8,000	$4,800	$12,800	$1,067	$160,000
7	3%	$8,000	$4,320	$12,320	$1,027	$144,000
10	3%	$8,000	$3,600	$11,600	$967	$120,000
20	3%	$8,000	$1,200	$9,200	$767	$40,000
25	3%	$8,000	$240	$8,240	$687	$0
	5%					
1	5%	$8,000	$10,000	$18,000	$1,500	$192,000
2	5%	$8,000	$9,600	$17,600	$1,467	$186,000
5	5%	$8,000	$8,000	$16,000	$1,333	$160,000
7	5%	$8,000	$7,200	$15,200	$1,267	$144,000
10	5%	$8,000	$6,000	$14,000	$1,167	$120,000
20	5%	$8,000	$2,000	$10,000	$833	$40,000
25	5%	$8,000	$400	$8,400	$700	$0

		7%					
1		7%	$8,000	$14,000	$22,000	$1,833	$192,000
2		7%	$8,000	$13,440	$21,440	$1,787	$186,000
5		7%	$8,000	$11,200	$19,200	$1,600	$160,000
7		7%	$8,000	$10,080	$18,080	$1,507	$144,000
10		7%	$8,000	$8,400	$16,400	$1,367	$120,000
20		7%	$8,000	$2,800	$10,800	$900	$40,000
25		7%	$8,000	$560	$8,560	$713	$0
		10%					
1		10%	$8,000	$20,000	$28,000	$2,333	$192,000
2		10%	$8,000	$19,200	$27,200	$2,267	$186,000
5		10%	$8,000	$16,000	$24,000	$2,000	$160,000
7		10%	$8,000	$14,400	$22,400	$1,867	$144,000
10		10%	$8,000	$12,000	$20,000	$1,667	$120,000
20		10%	$8,000	$4,000	$12,000	$1,000	$40,000
25		10%	$8,000	$800	$8,800	$733	$0

If you withdraw your amount at the beginning of each year, you will deplete your funds in about 25 years (as depicted in this chart). If you take interest and principal out at the end of each year, you will deplete your funds in about 26 years. If your withdrawals are monthly, then your depletion will occur somewhere between 25 and 26 years. Too, if the interest rate you are paid over time varies, your depletion point may be shorter or longer, depending on, respectively, if the interest rate declines or increases.

Appendix 2

Projected Retirement Payouts for a Defined-Benefit Pension Plan

Percentage	Years of Service	Average salary	Annual benefit	Monthly benefit
2%	10	$25,000	$5000	$417
2.5%	15	$25,000	$9375	$781
2.6%	25	$30,000	$19,000	$1624

Appendix 3

Civil Service Retirement System (CSRS) Retirement Benefit Based on

$50,000 Annual Salary and 25 Years of Service

First 5 years	.015 x $50,000 x 5	$3750		
Next 5 years	.0175 x $50,000 x 5	$4375		
Remaining 15 years	.02 x $50,000 x 15	$15,000		
Total Benefit per year			$23125	
Benefit per month				$1927

Appendix 4

Federal Employees Retirement System (FERS) Retirement Benefit

Based on $50,000 Annual Salary and 25 Years of Service

Years of Service	Calculation	Retirement Benefit
25 years of service	.011 x $50,000 x 25	$13750

Appendix 5

Social Security Benefits Relative to Birth Year

With Projected Reductions

Retirement age	Monthly benefit
65 (born 1937 or earlier)	$1000
*62 (born 1937 or earlier)	$800 (20% reduction)
67 (born 1960)	$1000
**62 (born 1960)	$700 (30% reduction)

*If full retirement age is 65, the entitlement is reduced by 5/9 of 1% for each month it is

taken before this time.

**If full retirement age is 67, the entitlement is reduced by 5/9 of 1% for the first 36 months and

5/12 of 1% for each subsequent month if it is taken before this time.

Appendix 6

Second Month Allocation and Accumulation for Hypothetical Budget

Budget Item	Allocation from Pool ($5000)	Month 1 Allocation	Month 1 Accumulation	Month 2 Allocation	Month 2 Accumulation
Allowance (Male)		$120	$120-$75-$20	$120	$145
Allowance (Female)		$120	$120-$120	$120	$120
Auto Insurance	$300	$75	$375	$75	$450
Auto License		$30	$30	$30	$60
Donations	$400	$300	$700-$500	$300	$500
Entertainment		$100	$100	$100	$200
Gasoline		$60	$60-$25-$25-$10	$60	$60
Gifts		$40	$40	$40	$80
Groceries		$400	$400-$150-$150-$100	$400	$400
Health Insurance	$500	$135	$635	$135	$770
House Insurance	$200	$100	$300	$100	$400
House Repairs	$50	$75	$125-$55	$75	$145
Income Tax		$150	$150	$150	$300
Long Term Health Ins	$500	$100	$600	$100	$700
Medicine	$100	$50	$150-$120	$50	$80
Miscellaneous		$100	$100-$70-$25	$100	$105
Mortgage	$2000	$1100	$3100-$1100	$1100	$3100

Payments					
Periodicals and Newspapers	$50	$25	$75	$25	$100
Property Tax	$500	$200	$700	$200	$900
Savings		$200	$200	$200	$400
Utilities	$300	$220	$520-460	$220	$280
Vacation and Travel	$100	$200	$300-$100	$200	$400
Totals	**$5000**	**$4000**	**$5635#**	**$4000##**	**$9635***

Appendix 7

Third Month Allocation and Accumulation for Hypothetical Budget

Budget Item	Allocation from Pool ($5000)	Month 1 Allocation	Month 1	Month 2 Allocation	Month 2	Month 3 Allocation	Month 3
Allowance (Male)		$120	$120-$75-$20	$120	$145	$120	
Allowance (Female)		$120	$120-$120	$120	$120	$120	
Auto Insurance	$300	$75	$375	$75	$450	$75	
Auto License		$30	$30	$30	$60	$30	
Donations	$400	$300	$700-$500	$300	$500	$300	
Entertainment		$100	$100	$100	$200	$100	
Gasoline		$60	$60-$25-$25-$10	$60	$60	$60	
Gifts		$40	$40	$40	$80	$40	
Groceries		$400	$400-$150-$150-$50	$400	$400	$400	
Health Insurance	$500	$135	$635	$135	$770	$135	
House Insurance	$200	$100	$300	$100	$400	$100	
House Repairs	$50	$75	$125-$55	$75	$145	$75	
Income Tax		$150	$150	$150	$300	$150	
Long Term Health Insurance	$500	$100	$600	$100	$700	$100	
Medicine	$100	$50	$150-$120	$50	$80	$50	
Miscellaneous		$100	$100-$70-$25	$100	$105	$100	

Mortgage Payments	$2,000	$1,100	$3100-$1100	$1,100	$4,000	$1,100	
Periodicals and Newspapers	$50	$25	$75	$25	$100	$25	
Property Tax	$500	$200	$700	$200	$900	$200	
Savings		$200	$200	$400	$200	$600	
Utilities	$300	$220	$520-460	$220	$280	$220	
Vacation and Travel	$100	$200	$300-$100	$200	$400	$200	
Totals	**$5,000**	**$4,000**	***	**$4,000**	***	**$4,000**	

The total of the past month (#) plus the current allocation (##) should equal what you have in your bank account. (***)

139

Appendix 8

Format for Listing Assets and Liabilities

Date	Assets and Liabilities	Value	Account #	Managing Agency
	House			
	Car 1			
	Car 2			
	Note Receivable			
	Annuity			
	Savings Account			
	Checking Account			
	Life Insurance Policy			
	IRA 1			
	IRA 2			
	403b			
	Utility Stock			
	CD (savings)			
	Total Assets	*		
	Liabilities (Debt)			
	Car Loan 2			
	Mortgage			
	Credit card debt			
	Total Liabilities	**		
	Total Value			
	(Assets-liabilities)			
	(* minus **)			

Appendix 9

Adjustment of Medicare Premium Based on Income

For 2016

Category	Modified Adjusted Gross Income	Cost $121.80 plus	Prescription Drug Coverage
Married, filing	$170,000.01 to $214,000	$48.70	$12.70
jointly	$214,000.01 to $320,000	$121.80	$32.80
	$320,000.01 to $428,000	$194.90	$52.80
	More than $428,000	$268	$72.90
Single,	$85,000.01 to $107,000	$48.70	$12.70
Head of	$107,000.01 to $160,000	$121.80	$32.80
Household,	$160,000.01 to $214,000	$194.90	$52.80
Qualified	More than $214,000	$268	$72.90
Widow(er)			
Married, filing separately	$85,000.01 to $129,000	$194.90	$52.80
	More than $129,000	$268	$72.90

141

Resources for Retirement Planning

Webography

Annuity Advantage

http://www.annuityadvantage.com/

This site unravels some of the issues involved with understanding various types of annuities and how they pay out.

A.A.R.P.

http://www.aarp.org/

This site includes numerous articles and links regarding retirement, including pending laws, volunteering, tax assistance and legal issues.

Best Places to Retire

http://money.cnn.com/best/bpretire/

This site is useful in assessing good areas in which to retire throughout the United States.

Center for Retirement Research

http://www.be.edu/centers/err/

This is an excellent site devoted to numerous retirement issues.

Five Retirement Must Knows

http://www.fool.com/Retirement/Retirement01.htm

The title says it all.

How Far Will My Salary Go In Another City?

http://cgi.money.cnn.com/tools/costofliving/costofliving.html?step=form

This page presents a useful tool for comparing costs between cities.

How to Retire in Style

http://www.fool.com/Retirement/RetirementPlanning/RetirementPlanning01.htm

From the Motley Fool, this site provides links to retirement issues related to taxes, Social Security, second careers, insurance and inheritances.

Internal Revenus Service

http://www.irs.gov/ This is a useful site for general information on Federal taxes as wells forms which can be downloaded.

Online Personal Guides to Investing

http://mutualfunds.troweprice.com/personalguide.html

This site provides guides for choosing a mutual fund, planning and rolling over a 401k or investing in an IRA.

Planning Your Estate http://www.fool.com/Retirement/Retirement04.htm
This site provides discussion on where to live and the rewards or pitfalls of working part-time.

Retirement and Wills
http://moneycentral.msn.com/retire/home.asp
This site provides several links to commentaries on retirement.

Retirement: Are You Ready for 100?
http://money.cnn.com/2006/01/05/pf/retirement_planning/index.htm
This article discusses increased life expectancy, how to calculate it as well as the implications for financial planning.

Retirement Essentials
http://money.cnn.com/retirement/
This site provides numerous and relevant links to retirement issues.

Retirement Living Information Center
 http://www.retirementliving.com/
This site provides information on retirement communities, places to retire, state taxes, retirement trends and issues, as well as state sting agencies.

Retirement Planner
http://cgi.money.cnn.com/tools/retirementplanner/retirementplanner.jsp
This page provides a useful tool for calculating what you may need to retire in the manner you wish.

Reverse Mortgage Loan Calculator
http://www.wellsrm.com/
This cite provides an estimate of benefits from three popular reverse mortgage programs.

Social Security Online
http://www.ssa.gov/
This is the definitive site for all issues related to Social Security Benefits, including calculating benefits, legal updates and medical/disability concerns.

State Tax Links
http://www.taxsites.com/state.html
This is a comprehensive site that provides link to the tax situation in each of the United States.

U.S. News & World Report on Retirement
 http://www.usnews.com/usnews/biztech/btretirement.htm
This site has articles on The Golden Years Grind, Medicare's Drug Plan, retirement cities, cashing out your pension, senior health and lifestyle.

Where to Invest Your Money
http://www.fool.com/Retirement/Retirement02.htm
This is a comprehensive site that enumerates and explains various instruments for building retirement savings.